AF348588

NIHILISM

The Root of the Revolution of the Modern Age

Eugene (Fr. Seraphim) Rose

ST. HERMAN OF ALASKA BROTHERHOOD
2026

Copyright © 1994, 2026 by the St. Herman of Alaska Brotherhood
All rights reserved

Address all correspondence to:
St. Herman of Alaska Brotherhood
P. O. Box 70
Platina, CA 96076

www.sainthermanmonastery.com

First Printing: 1994
Second Printing: 1995
Second Edition, Third Printing: 2001
Second Edition, Fourth Printing: 2009
Second Edition, Fifth Printing: 2018
Second Edition, Sixth Printing: 2020
Second Edition, Seventh Printing: 2024
Second Edition, Eighth Printing: 2026

Front cover: calligraphy by John Burns

Printed in the United States of America

Publishers Cataloging in Publication

Rose, Eugene (Fr. Seraphim), 1934–1982
    Nihilism: the root of the revolution of the modern age.

Library of Congress Control Number: 2001092024
ISBN: 978-1-887904-06-3

CONTENTS

Fr. Seraphim Rose (1934–1982) at the St. Herman of Alaska Monastery in the mountains of the northern California. Photograph taken in 1982.

Editor's Preface

In a basement apartment near downtown San Francisco in the early 1960s, Eugene Rose, the future Fr. Seraphim, sat at his desk covered with stacks of books and piles of paper folders. The room was perpetually dark, for little light could come in from the window. Some years before Eugene had moved there, a murder had occurred in that room, and some said that an ominous spirit still lingered there. But Eugene, as if in defiance of this spirit and the ever-darkening spirit of the city around him, had one wall covered with icons, before which a red icon-lamp always flickered.

In this room Eugene undertook to write a monumental chronicle of modern man's war against God, his attempt to destroy the Old Order and raise up a new one without Christ, to deny the existence of the Kingdom of God and raise up his own earthly utopia in its stead. This projected work was entitled *The Kingdom of Man and the Kingdom of God.*

Only a few years before this, Eugene himself had been ensnared in the Kingdom of Man and had suffered in it; he too had been at war against God. Having rejected the Protestant Christianity of his formative years as being weak and ineffectual, he had taken part in the Bohemian counterculture of the 1950s, and had delved into Eastern religions and philosophies which taught that God is ultimately impersonal. Like the absurdist artists and writers of his day, he had experimented with insanity, breaking down logical thought processes as a way of "breaking on through to the other side." He read the words of the mad "prophet" of Nihilism, Friedrich Nietzsche, until those words resonated in his soul with an electric, infernal power. Through all these means, he was seeking to attain to Truth or Reality with his mind; but they all resulted in failure. He was reduced to such a state of despair that, when later asked to describe it, he could only say, "I was in Hell." He would get drunk, and would grapple with the God Whom he had claimed was dead, pounding on the floor and screaming at Him to leave him alone. Once while intoxicated, he wrote, "I am sick, as all men are sick who are absent from the love of God."

"Atheism," Eugene wrote in later years, "true 'existential' atheism burning with hatred of a seemingly unjust or unmerciful God, is a spiritual state; it is a real attempt to grapple with the true God Whose ways are so inexplicable even to the most believing of men, and it has more than once been known to end in a blinding vision of Him Whom the real atheist truly seeks. It is Christ Who works in these souls. The Antichrist is not to be found primarily in the great deniers, but in the small affirmers, whose Christ is only on the lips. Nietzsche, in calling himself Antichrist, proved thereby his intense hunger for Christ...."

It was in such a condition of intense hunger that Eugene found himself in the late 1950s. And then, like a sudden gust of wind, there entered into his life a reality that he never could have foreseen. Towards the end of his life he recalled this moment:

"For years in my studies I was satisfied with being 'above all traditions' but somehow faithful to them.... When I visited an Orthodox church, it was only in order to view another 'tradition.' However, when I entered an Orthodox church for the first time (a Russian church in San Francisco) something happened to me that I had not experienced in any Buddhist or other Eastern temple; something in my heart said that this was 'home,' that all my search was over. I didn't really know what this meant, because the service was quite strange to me, and in a foreign language. I began to attend Orthodox services more frequently, gradually learning its language and customs.... With my exposure to Orthodoxy and to Orthodox people, a new idea began to enter my awareness: that Truth was not just an abstract idea, sought and known by the mind, but was something personal—even a

Person—sought and loved by the heart. And that is how I met Christ."

WHILE working on *The Kingdom of Man and the Kingdom of God* in his basement apartment, Eugene was still coming to grips with what he had found. He had come upon the Truth in the Undistorted Image of Christ, as preserved in the Eastern Orthodox Church, but he yearned to enter into what he called the "heart of hearts" of that Church, its mystical dimension. He wanted God, and wanted Him desperately. His writings from this time were a kind of catharsis for him: a means of *emerging* out of untruth, out of the underground darkness and into the light. Although they are philosophical in tone, much more so than his later works, these early writings were born of an intense suffering that was still very fresh in his soul. It was only natural that he would write much more about the Kingdom of Man, in which he had suffered all his life, than about the Kingdom of God, of which he had as yet only caught a glimpse. It was still through the prism of the Kingdom of Man that he viewed the Kingdom of God.

Of all the fourteen chapters Eugene planned to write for his *magnum opus* (see the outline on p. 100), only the seventh was typed in completed form; the rest remain in handwritten notes. This seventh chapter, which we present below, was on the philosophy of Nihilism.

Nihilism—the belief that there is no Absolute Truth, that all truth is relative—is, Eugene affirmed, *the* basic philosophy of the 20th century: "It has become, in our time, so widespread and pervasive, has entered so thoroughly and so deeply into the minds and hearts of all men living today, that there is no longer any 'front' on which it may be fought." The heart of this philosophy, he said, was "expressed most clearly by Nietzsche and by a character of Dostoyevsky in the phrase: 'God is dead, therefore man becomes God and everything is possible.'"

From his own experience, Eugene believed that modern man cannot come to Christ fully until he is first aware of how far he and his society have fallen away from Him, that is, until he has first faced the

Nihilism in himself. "The Nihilism of our age exists in all," he wrote, "and those who do not, with the aid of God, choose to combat it in the name of the fullness of Being of the living God, are swallowed up in it already. We have been brought to the edge of the abyss of nothingness and, whether we recognize its nature or not, we will, through affinity for the ever-present nothingness within us, be engulfed in it beyond all hope of redemption—unless we cling in full and certain faith (which, doubting, does not doubt) to Christ, without Whom we are truly nothing."

As a writer, Eugene felt he must call his contemporaries back from the abyss. He wrote not only out of his own desire for God, but out of his concern for others who desired Him also—even those who, as he himself had once done, rejected God or warred against Him out of their very desire for Him.

Out of his pain of heart, out of the darkness of his former life, Eugene speaks to contemporary humanity which finds itself in the same pain and darkness. Now, nearly half a century since he wrote this work, as the powers of Nihilism and anti-Christianity enter more deeply into the fiber of our society, his words are more needed than ever. Having faced and fought against the Nihilism in himself, he is able to help prevent us from being captured by its soul-destroying spirit, and to help us cling to Christ, the Eternal Truth become flesh.

—Hieromonk Damascene (Christensen)
St. Herman of Alaska Monastery

I. Introduction:

The Question of Truth

WHAT is the Nihilism in which we have seen the root of the Revolution of the modern age? The answer, at first thought, does not seem difficult; several obvious examples of it spring immediately to mind. There is Hitler's fantastic program of destruction, the Bolshevik Revolution, the Dadaist attack on art; there is the background from which these movements sprang, most notably represented by several "possessed" individuals of the late nineteenth century—poets like Rimbaud and Baudelaire, revolutionaries like Bakunin and Nechayev, "prophets" like Nietzsche; there is, on a humbler level among our contemporaries, the vague unrest that leads some to flock to magicians like Hitler, and others to find escape in drugs or false religions, or to perpetrate those "senseless" crimes that become ever more characteristic of these times. But these represent no more than the spectacular surface of the problem of Nihilism. To account even for these, once one probes beneath the surface, is by no means an easy task; but the task we have set for ourselves in this chapter is broader: to understand the nature of the whole movement of which these phenomena are but extreme examples.

To do this it will be necessary to avoid two great pitfalls lying on either side of the path we have chosen, into one or the other of which most commentators on the Nihilist spirit of our age have fallen: apology, and diatribe.

Anyone aware of the too-obvious imperfections and evils of modern civilization that have been the more immediate occasion and cause of the Nihilist reaction—though we shall see that these too have been the fruit of an incipient Nihilism—cannot but feel a measure of sympathy with some, at least, of the men who have participated in that reaction. Such sympathy may take the form of pity for men who may, from one point of view, be seen as innocent "victims" of the conditions against which their effort has been directed; or again, it may be expressed in the common opinion that certain types of Nihilist phenomena have actually a "positive" significance and have a role to play in some "new development" of history or of man. The latter attitude, again, is itself one of the more obvious fruits of the very Nihilism in question here; but the former attitude, at least, is not entirely devoid of truth or justice. For that very reason, however, we must be all the more careful not to give it undue importance. It is all too easy, in the atmosphere of intellectual fog that pervades Liberal and Humanist circles today, to allow sympathy for an unfortunate person to pass over into receptivity to his ideas. The Nihilist, to be sure, is in some sense "sick," and his sickness is a testimony to the sickness of an age whose best—as well as worst—elements turn to Nihilism; but sickness is not cured, nor even properly diagnosed by "sympathy." In any case there is no such thing as an entirely "innocent victim." The Nihilist is all too obviously involved in the very sins and guilt of mankind that have produced the evils of our age; and in taking arms—as do all Nihilists—not only against real or imagined "abuses" and "injustices" in the social and religious order, but also against order itself and the Truth that underlies that order, the Nihilist takes an active part in the work of Satan (for such it is) that can by no means be explained away by the mythology of the "innocent victim." No one, in the last analysis, serves Satan against his will.

But if "apology" is far from our intention in these pages, neither is our aim mere diatribe. It is not sufficient, for example, to condemn

Naziism or Bolshevism for their "barbarism," "gangsterism," or "anti-intellectualism," and the artistic or literary avant-garde for their "pessimism" or "exhibitionism"; nor is it enough to defend the "democracies" in the name of "civilization," "progress," or "humanism," or for their advocacy of "private property" or "civil liberties." Such arguments, while some of them possess a certain justice, are really quite beside the point; the blows of Nihilism strike too deep, its program is far too radical, to be effectively countered by them. Nihilism has error for its root, and error can be conquered only by Truth. Most of the criticism of Nihilism is not directed to this root at all, and the reason for this—as we shall see—is that Nihilism has become, in our time, so widespread and pervasive, has entered so thoroughly and so deeply into the minds and hearts of all men living today, that there is no longer any "front" on which it may be fought; and those who think they are fighting it are most often using its own weapons, which they in effect turn against themselves.

Some will perhaps object—once they have seen the scope of our project—that we have set our net too wide: that we have exaggerated the prevalence of Nihilism or, if not, then that the phenomenon is so universal as to defy handling at all. We must admit that our task is an ambitious one, all the more so because of the ambiguity of many Nihilist phenomena; and indeed, if we were to attempt a thorough examination of the question our work would never end.

It is possible, however, to set our net wide and still catch the fish we are after—because it is, after all, a single fish, and a large one. A complete documentation of Nihilist phenomena is out of the question; but an examination of the unique Nihilist mentality that underlies them, and of its indisputable effects and its role in contemporary history, is surely possible.

We shall attempt here, first, to describe this mentality—in several, at least, of its most important manifestations—and offer a sketch of its historical development; and then to probe more deeply into its meaning and historical program. But before this can be done, we must know more clearly of what we are speaking; we must begin, therefore, with a definition of Nihilism.

This task need not detain us long; Nihilism has been defined, and quite succinctly, by the fount of philosophical Nihilism, Nietzsche.

"That there is *no truth;* that there is no absolute state of affairs—no 'thing-in-itself.' *This alone is Nihilism, and of the most extreme kind."**

"There is no truth": we have encountered this phrase already more than once in this book, and it will recur frequently hereafter. For the question of Nihilism is, most profoundly, a question of truth; it is, indeed, *the* question of truth.

But what is truth? The question is, first of all, one of logic: before we discuss the content of truth, we must examine its very possibility, and the conditions of its postulation. And by "truth" we mean, of course—as Nietzsche's denial of it makes explicit—absolute truth, which we have already defined as the dimension of the beginning and the end of things.

"Absolute truth": the phrase has, to a generation raised on skepticism and unaccustomed to serious thought, an antiquated ring. No one, surely—is the common idea—no one is naive enough to believe in "absolute truth" any more; all truth, to our enlightened age, is "relative." The latter expression, let us note—"all truth is relative"—is the popular translation of Nietzsche's phrase, "there is no (absolute) truth"; the one doctrine is the foundation of the Nihilism alike of the masses and of the elite.

"Relative truth" is primarily represented, for our age, by the knowledge of science, which begins in observation, proceeds by logic, and progresses in orderly fashion from the known to the unknown. It is always discursive, contingent, qualified, always expressed in "relation" to something else, never standing alone, never categorical, never "absolute."

* *The Will to Power,* Vol. I, in *The Complete Works of Friedrich Nietzsche,* New York, The Macmillan Company, 1909, Vol. 14, p. 6.

The unreflective scientific specialist sees no need for any other kind of knowledge; occupied with the demands of his specialty, he has, perhaps, neither time nor inclination for "abstract" questions that inquire, for example, into the basic presuppositions of that specialty. If he is pressed, or if his mind spontaneously turns to such questions, the most obvious explanation is usually sufficient to satisfy his curiosity: all truth is empirical, all truth is relative.

Either statement, of course, is a self-contradiction. The first statement is itself not empirical at all, but metaphysical; the second is itself an absolute statement. The question of absolute truth is raised first of all, for the critical observer, by such self-contradictions; and the first logical conclusion to which he must be led is this: if there is any truth at all, it cannot be merely "relative." The first principles of modern science, as of any system of knowledge, are themselves unchangeable and absolute; if they were not there would be no knowledge at all, not even the most "reflective" knowledge, for there would be no criteria by which to classify anything as knowledge or truth.

This axiom has a corollary: the absolute cannot be attained by means of the relative. That is to say, the first principles of any system of knowledge cannot be arrived at through the means of that knowledge itself, but must be given in advance; they are the object, not of scientific demonstration, but of faith.

We have discussed, in an earlier chapter, the universality of faith, seeing it as underlying all human activity and knowledge; and we have seen that faith, if it is not to fall prey to subjective delusions, must be rooted in truth. It is therefore a legitimate, and indeed unavoidable question whether the first principles of the scientific faith—for example, the coherence and uniformity of nature, the transsubjectivity of human knowledge, the adequacy of reason to draw conclusions from observation—are founded in absolute truth; if they are not, they can be no more than unverifiable probabilities. The "pragmatic" position taken by many scientists and humanists who cannot be troubled to think about ultimate things—the position that these principles are no more than experimental hypotheses which collective experience finds reliable—is surely unsatisfactory; it may offer a psychological explanation of the faith these principles inspire, but since it does not establish the foundation of that faith in truth, it leaves the whole scientific edifice on shifting sands and provides no sure defense against the irrational winds that periodically attack it.

In actual fact, however,—whether it be from simple naivete or from a deeper insight which they cannot justify by argument—most scientists and humanists undoubtedly believe that their faith has something to do with the truth of things. Whether this belief is justified or not is, of course, another question; it is a metaphysical question, and one thing that is certain is that it is *not* justified by the rather primitive metaphysics of most scientists.

Every man, as we have seen, lives by faith; likewise every man—something less obvious but no less certain—is a metaphysician. The claim to any knowledge whatever—and no living man can refrain from this claim—implies a theory and standard of knowledge, and a notion of what is ultimately knowable and true. This ultimate truth, whether it be conceived as the Christian God or simply as the ultimate coherence of things, is a metaphysical first principle, an absolute truth. But with the acknowledgement, logically unavoidable, of such a principle, the theory of the "relativity of truth" collapses, it itself being revealed as a self-contradictory absolute.

The proclamation of the "relativity of truth" is, thus, what might be called a "negative metaphysics"—but a metaphysics all the same. There are several principal forms of "negative metaphysics," and since each contradicts itself in a slightly different way, and appeals to a slightly different mentality, it would be wise to devote a paragraph here to the examination of each. We may divide them into the two general categories of "realism" and "agnosticism," each of which in turn may be subdivided into "naive" and "critical."

"Naive realism," or "naturalism," does not precisely deny absolute truth, but rather makes absolute claims of its own that cannot be defended. Rejecting any "ideal" or "spiritual" absolute, it claims the absolute truth of "materialism" and "determinism." This philosophy is still current in some circles—it is official Marxist doctrine and is expounded by some unsophisticated scientific thinkers in the West—but the main current of contemporary thought has left it behind, and it seems today the quaint relic of a simpler, but bygone, day, the Victorian day when many transferred to "science" the allegiance and emotions they had once devoted to religion. It is the impossible formulation of a "scientific" metaphysics—impossible because science is, by its nature, knowledge of the particular, and metaphysics is knowledge of what underlies the particular and is presupposed by it. It is a suicidal philosophy in that the "materialism" and "determinism" it posits render all philosophy invalid; since it must insist that philosophy, like everything else, is "determined," its advocates can only claim that their philosophy, since it exists, is "inevitable," but not at all that it is "true." This philosophy, in fact, if consistent, would do away with the category of truth altogether; but its adherents, innocent of thought that is either consistent or profound, seem unaware of this fatal contradiction. The contradiction may be seen, on a less abstract level, in the altruistic and idealistic practice of, for example, the Russian Nihilists of the last century, a practice in flagrant contradiction of their purely materialistic and egoistic theory; Vladimir Solovyov cleverly pointed out this discrepancy by ascribing to them the syllogism, "Man is descended from a monkey, consequently we shall love one another."

All philosophy presupposes, to some degree, the autonomy of ideas; philosophical "materialism" is, thus, a species of "idealism." It is, one might say, the self-confession of those whose ideas do not rise above the obvious, whose thirst for truth is so easily assuaged by science that they make it into their absolute.

"Critical realism," or "positivism," is the straightforward denial of metaphysical truth. Proceeding from the same scientific predispositions as the more naive naturalism, it professes greater modesty in abandoning the absolute altogether and restricting itself to "empirical," "relative" truth. We have already noted the contradiction in this position: the denial of absolute truth is itself an "absolute truth"; again, as with naturalism, the very positing of the first principle of positivism is its own refutation.

"Agnosticism," like "realism," may be distinguished as "naive" and "critical." "Naive" or "doctrinaire agnosticism" posits the absolute unknowability of any absolute truth. While its claim seems more modest even than that of positivism, it still quite clearly claims too much: if it actually *knows* that the absolute is "unknowable," then this knowledge is itself "absolute." Such agnosticism is in fact but a variety of positivism, attempting, with no greater success, to cover up its contradictions.

Only in "critical" or "pure agnosticism" do we find, at last, what seems to be a successful renunciation of the absolute; unfortunately, such renunciation entails the renunciation of everything else and ends—if it is consistent—in total solipsism. Such agnosticism is the simple statement of fact: we do not know whether there exists an absolute truth, or what its nature could be if it did exist; let us, then—this is the corollary—content ourselves with the empirical, relative truth we *can* know. But what is truth? What is knowledge? If there is no absolute standard by which these are to be measured, they cannot even be defined. The agnostic, if he acknowledges this criticism, does not allow it to disturb him; his position is one of "pragmatism," "experimentalism," "instrumentalism": there is no truth, but man can survive, can get along in the world, without it. Such a position has been defended in high places—and in very low places as well—in our anti-intellectualist century; but the least one can say of it is that it is intellectually irresponsible. It is the definitive abandonment of truth, or rather the surrender of truth to power, whether that power be nation, race, class, comfort, or whatever other cause is able to absorb the energies men once devoted to the truth.

The "pragmatist" and the "agnostic" may be quite sincere and well-meaning; but they only deceive themselves—and others—if they continue to use the word "truth" to describe what they are seeking. Their existence, in fact, is testimony to the fact that the search for truth which has so long animated European man has come to an end. Four centuries and more of modern thought have been, from one point of view, an experiment in the possibilities of knowledge open to man, assuming that *there is no Revealed Truth.* The conclusion—which Hume already saw and from which he fled into the comfort of "common sense" and conventional life, and which the multitudes sense today without possessing any such secure refuge—the conclusion of this experiment is an absolute negation: if there is no Revealed Truth, there is no truth at all; the search for truth outside of Revelation has come to a dead end. The scientist admits this by restricting himself to the narrowest of specialties, content if he sees a certain coherence in a limited aggregate of facts, without troubling himself over the existence of any truth, large or small; the multitudes demonstrate it by looking to the scientist, not for truth, but for the technological applications of a knowledge which has no more than a practical value, and by looking to other, irrational sources for the ultimate values men once expected to find in truth. The despotism of science over practical life is contemporaneous with the advent of a whole series of pseudo-religious "revelations"; the two are correlative symptoms of the same malady: the abandonment of truth.

Logic, thus, can take us this far: denial or doubt of absolute truth leads (if one is consistent and honest) to the abyss of solipsism and irrationalism; the only position that involves no *logical* contradictions is the affirmation of an absolute truth which underlies and secures all lesser truths; and this absolute truth can be attained by no relative, human means. At this point logic fails us, and we must enter an entirely different universe of discourse if we are to proceed. It is one thing to state that there is no logical barrier to the affirmation of absolute truth; it is quite another actually to affirm it. Such an affirmation can be based upon only one source; the question of truth must come in the end to the question of Revelation.

The critical mind hesitates at this point. Must we seek from without what we cannot attain by our own unaided power? It is a blow to pride—most of all to that pride which passes today for scientific "humility" that "sits down before fact as a little child" and yet refuses to acknowledge any arbiter of fact save the proud human reason. It is, however, a particular revelation—Divine Revelation, the Christian Revelation—that so repels the rationalist; other revelations he does not gainsay.

Indeed, the man who does not accept, fully and consciously, a coherent doctrine of truth such as the Christian Revelation provides, is forced—if he has any pretensions to knowledge whatever—to seek such a doctrine elsewhere; this has been the path of modern philosophy, which has ended in obscurity and confusion because it would never squarely face the fact that it cannot supply for itself what can only be given from without. The blindness and confusion of modern philosophers with regard to first principles and the dimension of the absolute have been the direct consequence of their own primary assumption, the non-existence of Revelation; for this assumption in effect blinded men to the light of the sun and rendered obscure everything that had once been clear in its light.

To one who gropes in this darkness there is but one path, if he will not be healed of his blindness; and that is to seek some light amidst the darkness here below. Many run to the flickering candle of "common sense" and conventional life and accept—because one must get along somehow—the current opinions of the social and intellectual circles to which they belong. But many others, finding this light too dim, flock to the magic lanterns that project beguiling, multicolored views that are, if nothing else, distracting; they become devotees of this or the other political or religious or artistic current that the "spirit of the age" has thrown into fashion.

In fact no one lives but by the light of some revelation, be it a true or a false one, whether it serve to enlighten or obscure. He who will not live by the Christian Revelation must live by a false revelation; and all false revelations lead to the Abyss.

We began this investigation with the logical question, "what is truth?" That question may—and must—be framed from an entirely different point of view. The skeptic Pilate asked the question, though not in earnest; ironically for him, he asked it of the Truth Himself. "I am the Way, the Truth, and the Life: no man cometh unto the Father, but by Me."* "Ye shall know the Truth, and the Truth shall make you free."** Truth in this sense, Truth that confers eternal life and freedom, cannot be attained by any human means; it can only be revealed from above by One Who has the power to do so.

The path to this Truth is a narrow one, and most men—because they travel the "broad" path—miss it. There is no man, however,—for so the God Who is Truth created him—who does not seek this Truth. We shall examine, in later chapters, many of the false absolutes, the false gods men have invented and worshipped in our idolatrous age; and we shall find that what is perhaps most striking about them is that every one of them, far from being any "new revelation," is a dilution, a distortion, a perversion, or a parody of the One Truth men cannot help but point to even in their error and blasphemy and pride. The notion of Divine Revelation has been thoroughly discredited for those who must obey the dictates of the "spirit of the age"; but it is impossible to extinguish the thirst for truth which God has implanted in man to lead them to Him, and which can only be satisfied in the acceptance of His Revelation. Even those who profess satisfaction with "relative" truths and consider themselves too "sophisticated" or "honest" or even "humble" to pursue the absolute—even they tire, eventually, of the fare of unsatisfying tidbits to which they have arbitrarily confined themselves, and long for more substantial fare.

The whole food of Christian Truth, however, is accessible only to faith; and the chief obstacle to such faith is not logic, as the facile modern view has it, but another and opposed faith. We have seen indeed, that logic cannot deny absolute truth without denying itself; the logic

* St. John XIV, 6.
** St. John VIII, 32.

that sets itself up against the Christian Revelation is merely the servant of another "revelation," of a false "absolute truth": namely Nihilism.

In the following pages we shall characterize as "Nihilists" men of, as it seems, widely divergent views: humanists, skeptics, revolutionaries of all hues, artists and philosophers of various schools; but they are united in a common task. Whether in positivist "criticism" of Christian truths and institutions, revolutionary violence against the Old Order, apocalyptic visions of universal destruction and the advent of a paradise on earth, or objective scientific labors in the interests of a "better life" in this world—the tacit assumption being that there is no other world—their aim is the same: the annihilation of Divine Revelation and the preparation of a new order in which there shall be no trace of the "old" view of things, in which Man shall be the only god there is.

II.

The Stages of the Nihilist Dialectic

THE Nihilist mentality, in the unity of its underlying aim, is single; but this mentality manifests itself in phenomena as diverse as the natures of the men who share it. The single Nihilist cause is thus advanced on many fronts simultaneously, and its enemies are confused and deceived by this effective tactic. To the careful observer, however, Nihilist phenomena reduce themselves to three or four principal types, and these few types are, further, related to each other as stages in a process which may be called the Nihilist dialectic. One stage of Nihilism opposes itself to another, not to combat it effectively, but to incorporate its errors into its own program and carry mankind one step further on the road to the Abyss that lies at the end of all Nihilism. The arguments at each stage, to be sure, are often effective in pointing out certain obvious deficiencies of a preceding or succeeding stage; but no criticism is ever radical enough to touch on the common errors all stages share, and the partial truths which are admittedly present in all forms of Nihilism are in the end only tactics to seduce men to the great falsehood that underlies them all.

The stages to be described in the following pages are not to be understood as merely chronological, though in the narrowest sense they are in fact a kind of chronicle of the development of the Nihilist mentality from the time of the failure of the Nihilist experiment of the French Revolution to the rise and fall of the latest and most explicitly Nihilist manifestation of the Revolution, National Socialism. Thus the two decades before and the two after the middle of the nineteenth century may be seen as the summit of Liberal prestige and influence, and J. S. Mill as the typical Liberal; the age of Realism occupies perhaps the last half of the century and is exemplified on the one hand by socialist thinkers, on the other by the philosophers and popularizers (we should perhaps rather say "exploiters") of science; Vitalism, in the forms of Symbolism, occultism, artistic Expressionism, and various evolutionary and "mystical" philosophies, is the most significant intellectual undercurrent throughout the half century after about 1875; and the Nihilism of Destruction, though its intellectual roots lie deep in the preceding century, brings to a grand conclusion, in the public order as well as in many private spheres, the whole century and a quarter of Nihilist development with the concentrated era of destruction of 1914–1945.

It will be noticed that these periods overlap, for Nihilism matures at a different rate in different peoples and in different individuals; the overlapping in fact is more extreme than our simple scheme can suggest, so much so that representatives of every stage can be found in every period, and all of them exist contemporaneously even today. What is true of historical periods is true also of individuals; there is no such thing as a "pure" Nihilist at any stage, every predominantly Nihilist temperament being a combination of at least two of the stages.

Further, if the age since the French Revolution is the first one in which Nihilism has played the central role, each of its stages has been represented in earlier centuries. Liberalism, for example, is a direct derivative of Renaissance Humanism; Realism was an important aspect of the Protestant Reformation as well as of the French Enlightenment; a kind of Vitalism appeared in Renaissance and Enlightenment occultism and again in Romanticism; and the Nihilism of Destruction, while never so thorough as it has been for the past century, has existed as a temptation for certain extremist thinkers throughout the modern age.

With these reservations, however, our scheme may perhaps be accepted as at least an approximation to what has been an undeniable historical and psychological process. Let us, then, begin our investigation of the stages of this process, the Nihilist dialectic, attempting to judge them by the clear light of the Orthodox Christian Truth which—if we are correct—they exist to obscure and deny. In this section we shall attempt no more than to describe these stages, and to point out, by reference to the definition of Nihilism we have adopted, in what respect they may be characterized as Nihilist.

1. LIBERALISM

The Liberalism we shall describe in the following pages is not—let us state at the outset—an overt Nihilism; it is rather a passive Nihilism, or, better yet, the neutral breeding-ground of the more advanced stages of Nihilism. Those who have followed our earlier discussion concerning the impossibility of spiritual or intellectual "neutrality" in this world will understand immediately why we have classified as Nihilist a point of view which, while not directly responsible for any striking Nihilist phenomena, has been an indispensable prerequisite for their appearance. The incompetent defence by Liberalism of a heritage in which it has never fully believed, has been one of the most potent causes of overt Nihilism.

The Liberal humanist civilization which, in Western Europe, was the last form of the Old Order that was effectively destroyed in the Great War and the Revolutions of the second decade of this century,* and which continues to exist—though in an even more attenuated, "democratic" form—in the free world today, may be principally characterized by its attitude to truth. This is not an attitude of open hostility nor even of deliberate unconcern, for its sincere apologists undeniably have a genuine regard for what they consider to be truth; rather, it is an attitude in which truth, despite certain appearances, no longer occupies the center of attention. The truth in which it professes to believe (apart,

* I.e., the twentieth century.—Ed.

of course, from scientific fact) is, for it, no spiritual or intellectual coin of current circulation, but idle and unfruitful capital left over from a previous age. The Liberal still speaks, at least on formal occasions, of "eternal verities," of "faith," of "human dignity," of man's "high calling" or his "unquenchable spirit," even of "Christian civilization"; but it is quite clear that these words no longer mean what they once meant. No Liberal takes them with entire seriousness; they are in fact metaphors, ornaments of language that are meant to evoke an emotional, not an intellectual, response—a response largely conditioned by long usage, with the attendant memory of a time when such words actually had a positive and serious meaning.

No one today who prides himself on his "sophistication"—that is to say, very few in academic institutions, in government, in science, in humanist intellectual circles, no one who wishes or professes to be abreast of the "times"—does or can fully believe in absolute truth, or more particularly in Christian Truth. Yet the name of truth has been retained, as have been the names of those truths men once regarded as absolute, and few in any position of authority or influence would hesitate to use them, even when they are aware that their meanings have changed. Truth, in a word, has been "reinterpreted"; the old forms have been emptied and given a new, quasi-Nihilist content. This may easily be seen by a brief examination of several of the principal areas in which truth has been "reinterpreted."

In the theological order the first truth is, of course, God. Omnipotent and omnipresent Creator of all, revealed to faith and in the experience of the faithful (and not contradicted by the reason of those who do not deny faith), God is the supreme end of all creation and Himself, unlike His creation, finds His end in Himself; everything created stands in relation to and dependence upon Him, Who alone depends upon nothing outside Himself; He has created the world that it might live in enjoyment of Him, and everything in the world is oriented toward this end, which however men may miss by a misuse of their freedom.

The modern mentality cannot tolerate such a God. He is both too intimate—too "personal," even too "human"—and too absolute, too uncompromising in His demands of us; and He makes Himself known only to humble faith—a fact bound to alienate the proud modern intelligence. A "new god" is clearly required by modern man, a god more closely fashioned after the pattern of such central modern concerns as science and business; it has, in fact, been an important intention of modern thought to provide such a god. This intention is clear already in Descartes, it is brought to fruition in the Deism of the Enlightenment, developed to its end in German idealism: the new god is not a Being but an idea, not revealed to faith and humility but constructed by the proud mind that still feels the need for "explanation" when it has lost its desire for salvation. This is the dead god of philosophers who require only a "first cause" to complete their systems, as well as of "positive thinkers" and other religious sophists who invent a god because they "need" him, and then think to "use" him at will. Whether "deist," "idealist," "pantheist," or "immanentist," all the modern gods are the same mental construct, fabricated by souls dead from the loss of faith in the true God.

The atheist arguments against such a god are as irrefutable as they are irrelevant; for such a god is, in fact, the same as no god at all. Uninterested in man, powerless to act in the world (except to inspire a worldly "optimism"), he is a god considerably weaker than the men who invented him. On such a foundation, needless to say, nothing secure can be built; and it is with good reason that Liberals, while usually professing belief in this deity, actually build their world-view upon the more obvious, though hardly more stable, foundation of Man. Nihilist atheism is the explicit formulation of what was already, not merely implicit, but actually present in a confused form, in Liberalism.

The ethical implications of belief in such a god are precisely the same as those of atheism; this inner agreement, however, is again disguised outwardly behind a cloud of metaphor. In the Christian order, all activity in this life is viewed and judged in the light of the life of the future world, the life beyond death which will have no end. The unbeliever can have no idea of what this life means to the believing Christian; for most people today the future life has, like God, become a mere idea, and it therefore costs as little pain and effort to deny as to affirm it. For the believing Christian, the future life is joy inconceivable, joy surpassing the joy he knows in this life through communion with God in prayer, in the Liturgy, in the Sacrament; because then God will be all in all and there will be no falling away from this joy, which will indeed be infinitely enhanced. The true believer has the consolation of a foretaste of eternal life. The believer in the modern god, having no such foretaste and hence no notion of Christian joy, cannot believe in the future life in the same way; indeed, if he were honest with himself, he would have to admit that he cannot believe in it at all.

There are two primary forms of such disbelief which passes for Liberal belief: the Protestant and the humanist. The Liberal Protestant view of the future life—shared, regrettably, by increasing numbers who profess to be Catholic or even Orthodox—is, like its views on everything else pertaining to the spiritual world, a minimal profession of faith that masks an actual faith in nothing. The future life has become a shadowy underworld in the popular conception of it, a place to take one's "deserved rest" after a life of toil. Nobody has a very clear idea of this realm, for it corresponds to no reality; it is rather an emotional projection, a consolation for those who would rather not face the implications of their actual disbelief.

Such a "heaven" is the fruit of a union of Christian terminology with ordinary worldliness, and it is convincing to no one who realizes that compromise in such ultimate matters is impossible; neither the true Orthodox Christian nor the consistent Nihilist is seduced by it. But the compromise of humanism is, if anything, even less convincing. Here there is scarcely even the pretense that the idea corresponds to reality; all becomes metaphor and rhetoric. The humanist no longer speaks of heaven at all, at least not seriously; but he does allow himself to speak of the "eternal," preferably in the form of a resounding figure of speech:

"eternal verities," "eternal spirit of men." One may justly question whether the word has any meaning at all in such phrases. In humanist stoicism the "eternal" has been reduced to a content so thin and frail as to be virtually indistinguishable from the materialist and determinist Nihilism that attempts—with some justification, surely—to destroy it.

In either case, in that of the Liberal "Christian" or the even more Liberal humanist, the inability to believe in eternal life is rooted in the same fact: they believe only in this world, they have neither experience nor knowledge of, nor faith in the other world, and most of all, they believe in a "god" *who is not powerful enough to raise men from the dead.*

Behind their rhetoric, the sophisticated Protestant and the humanist are quite aware that there is no room for Heaven, nor for eternity, in their universe; their thoroughly Liberal sensibility, again, looks not to a transcendent, but to an immanent source for its ethical doctrine, and their agile intelligence is even capable of turning this *faute de mieux* into a positive apology. It is—in this view—both "realism" and "courage" to live without hope of eternal joy nor fear of eternal pain; to one endowed with the Liberal view of things, it is not necessary to believe in Heaven or Hell to lead a "good life" in this world. Such is the total blindness of the Liberal mentality to the meaning of death.

If there is no immortality, the Liberal believes, one can still lead a civilized life; "if there is no immortality"—is the far profounder logic of Ivan Karamazov in Dostoyevsky's novel—"all things are lawful." Humanist stoicism is possible for certain individuals for a certain time: until, that is, the full implications of the denial of immortality strike home. The Liberal lives in a fool's paradise which must collapse before the truth of things. If death is, as the Liberal and Nihilist both believe, the extinction of the individual, then this world and everything in it—love, goodness, sanctity, everything—are as nothing, nothing man may do is of any ultimate consequence, and the full horror of life is hidden from man only by the strength of their will to deceive themselves; and "all things are lawful," no otherworldly hope or fear restrains men from monstrous experiments and suicidal dreams.

Nietzsche's words are the truth—and prophecy—of the new world that results from this view:

> Of all that which was formerly held to be true, not one word is to be credited. Everything which was formerly disdained as unholy, forbidden, contemptible, and fatal—all these flowers now bloom on the most charming paths of truth.*

The blindness of the Liberal is a direct antecedent of Nihilist, and more specifically of Bolshevist, morality; for the latter is only a consistent and systematic application of Liberal unbelief. It is the supreme irony of the Liberal view that it is precisely when its deepest intent shall have been realized in the world, and all men shall have been "liberated" from the yoke of transcendent standards, when even the pretense of belief in the other world shall have vanished—it is precisely then that life as the Liberal knows or desires it shall have become impossible; for the "new man" that disbelief produces can only see in Liberalism itself the last of the "illusions" which Liberalism wished to dispel.

In the Christian order politics too was founded upon absolute truth. We have already seen, in the preceding chapter, that the principal providential form government took in union with Christian Truth was the Orthodox Christian Empire, wherein sovereignty was vested in a Monarch, and authority proceeded from him downwards through a hierarchical social structure. We shall see in the next chapter, on the other hand, how a politics that rejects Christian Truth must acknowledge "the people" as sovereign and understand authority as proceeding from below upwards, in a formally "egalitarian" society. It is clear that one is the perfect inversion of the other; for they are opposed in their conceptions both of the source and of the end of government. Orthodox Christian Monarchy is government divinely established, and directed, ultimately, to the other world, government with the teaching of Christian Truth and the salvation of souls as its profoundest purpose; Nihilist rule—whose most fitting name, as we shall see, is Anarchy—is

* *The Will to Power,* p. 377.

government established by men, and directed solely to this world, government which has no higher aim than earthly happiness.

The Liberal view of government, as one might suspect, is an attempt at compromise between these two irreconcilable ideas. In the 19th century this compromise took the form of "constitutional monarchies," an attempt—again—to wed an old form to a new content; today the chief representatives of the Liberal idea are the "republics" and "democracies" of Western Europe and America, most of which preserve a rather precarious balance between the forces of authority and Revolution, while professing to believe in both.

It is of course impossible to believe in both with equal sincerity and fervor, and in fact no one has ever done so. Constitutional monarchs like Louis Philippe thought to do so by professing to rule "by the Grace of God and the will of the people"—a formula whose two terms annul each other, a fact as equally evident to the Anarchist* as to the Monarchist.

Now a government is secure insofar as it has God for its foundation and His Will for its guide; but this, surely, is not a description of Liberal government. It is, in the Liberal view, the people who rule, and not God; God Himself is a "constitutional monarch" Whose authority has been totally delegated to the people, and Whose function is entirely ceremonial. The Liberal believes in God with the same rhetorical fervor with which he believes in Heaven. The government erected upon such a faith is very little different, in principle, from a government erected upon total disbelief; and whatever its present residue of stability, it is clearly pointed in the direction of Anarchy.

A government must rule by the Grace of God *or* by the will of the people, it must believe in authority *or* in the Revolution; on these issues compromise is possible only in semblance, and only for a time. The Revolution, like the disbelief which has always accompanied it, cannot be stopped halfway; it is a force that, once awakened, will not rest until

* See, for example, Bakunin's remarks on Louis Napoleon in G. P. Maximoff, ed., *The Political Philosophy of Bakunin,* Glencoe, Illinois, The Free Press, 1953, p. 252.

it ends in a totalitarian Kingdom of this world. The history of the last two centuries has proved nothing if not this. To appease the Revolution and offer it concessions, as Liberals have always done, thereby showing that they have no truth with which to oppose it, is perhaps to postpone, but not to prevent, the attainment of its end. And to oppose the radical Revolution with a Revolution of one's own, whether it be "conservative," "non-violent," or "spiritual," is not merely to reveal ignorance of the full scope and nature of the Revolution of our time, but to concede as well the first principle of that Revolution: that the old truth is no longer true, and a new truth must take its place. Our next chapter will develop this point by defining more closely the goal of the Revolution.

In the Liberal world-view, therefore—in its theology, its ethics, its politics, and in other areas we have not examined as well—truth has been weakened, softened, compromised; in all realms truth that was once absolute has become less certain, if not entirely "relative." Now it is possible—and this in fact amounts to a definition of the Liberal enterprise—to preserve for a time the fruits of a system and a truth of which one is uncertain or skeptical; but one can build nothing positive upon such uncertainty, nor upon the attempt to make it intellectually respectable in the various relativistic doctrines we have already examined. There is and can be no philosophical apology for Liberalism; its apologies, when not simply rhetorical, are emotional and pragmatic. But the most striking fact about the Liberal, to any relatively unbiased observer, is not so much the inadequacy of his doctrine as his own seeming oblivion to this inadequacy.

This fact, which is understandably irritating to well-meaning critics of Liberalism, has only one plausible explanation. The Liberal is undisturbed even by fundamental deficiencies and contradictions in his own philosophy because his primary interest is elsewhere. If he is not concerned to found the political and social order upon Divine Truth, if he is indifferent to the reality of Heaven and Hell, if he conceives of God as a mere idea of a vague impersonal power, it is because he is more immediately interested in worldly ends, and because everything else is vague or abstract to him. The Liberal may be interested in culture, in learning, in business, or merely in comfort; but in every one of his pursuits the dimension of the absolute is simply absent. He is unable, or unwilling, to think in terms of ends, of ultimate things. The thirst for absolute truth has vanished; it has been swallowed up in worldliness.

In the Liberal universe, of course, truth—which is to say, learning—is quite compatible with worldliness; but there is more to truth than learning. "Every one that is of the truth heareth My voice."* No one has rightly sought the truth who has not encountered at the end of this search—whether to accept or reject Him—our Lord, Jesus Christ, "the Way, the Truth, and the Life," Truth that stands against the world and is a reproach to all worldliness. The Liberal, who thinks his universe secure against this Truth, is the "rich man" of the parable, over-burdened by his worldly interests and ideas, unwilling to give them up for the humility, poverty, and lowliness that are the marks of the genuine seeker after truth.

Nietzsche has given a second definition of Nihilism, or rather a commentary on the definition "there is no truth"; and that is, "there is no answer to the question: 'why?'"** Nihilism thus means that the ultimate questions have no answers, that is to say, no positive answers; and the Nihilist is he who accepts the implicit "no" the universe supposedly gives as its answer to these questions. But there are two ways of accepting this answer. There is the extreme path wherein it is made explicit and amplified in the programs of Revolution and destruction; this is Nihilism properly so-called, active Nihilism, for—in Nietzsche's words—"Nihilism is … not only the belief that everything deserves to perish; but one actually puts one's shoulder to the plough; *one destroys.*"*** But there is also a "moderate" path, which is that of the passive or implicit Nihilism we have been examining here, the Nihilism of the Liberal, the humanist, the agnostic who, agreeing that "there is no

* St. John XVIII, 37.
** *The Will to Power,* p. 8.
*** Ibid., p. 22.

truth," *no longer ask the ultimate questions.* Active Nihilism presupposes this Nihilism of skepticism and disbelief.

The totalitarian Nihilist regimes of this century have undertaken, as an integral part of their programs, the ruthless "reeducation" of their peoples. Few subjected to this process for any length of time have entirely escaped its influence; in a landscape where all is nightmare, one's sense of reality and truth inevitably suffers. A subtler "reeducation," quite humane in its means but nonetheless Nihilist in its consequences, has been practiced for some time in the free world, and nowhere more persistently or effectively than in its intellectual center, the academic world. Here external coercion is replaced by internal persuasion; a deadly skepticism reigns, hidden behind the remains of a "Christian heritage" in which few believe, and even fewer with deep conviction. The profound responsibility the scholar once possessed, the communication of truth, has been reneged; and all the pretended "humility" that seeks to conceal this fact behind sophisticated chatter on "the limits of human knowledge," is but another mask of the Nihilism the Liberal academician shares with the extremists of our day. Youth that—until it is "reeducated" in the academic environment—still thirsts for truth, is taught instead of truth the "history of ideas," or its interest is diverted into "comparative" studies, and the all-pervading relativism and skepticism inculcated in these studies is sufficient to kill in almost all the natural thirst for truth.

The academic world—and these words are neither lightly nor easily spoken—has become today, in large part, a source of corruption. It is corrupting to hear or read the words of men who do not believe in truth. It is yet more corrupting to receive, in place of truth, more learning and scholarship which, if they are presented as ends in themselves, are no more than parodies of the truth they were meant to serve, no more than a facade behind which there is no substance. It is, tragically, corrupting even to be exposed to the primary virtue still left to the academic world, the integrity of the best of its representatives—if this integrity serves, not the truth, but skeptical scholarship, and so seduces men all the more effectively to the gospel of subjectivism and unbelief this scholarship conceals. It is corrupting, finally, simply to live and work in an atmosphere totally permeated by a false conception of truth, wherein Christian Truth is seen as irrelevant to the central academic concerns, wherein even those who still believe this Truth can only sporadically make their voices heard above the skepticism promoted by the academic system. The evil, of course, lies primarily in the system itself, which is founded upon untruth, and only incidentally in the many professors whom this system permits and encourages to preach it.

The Liberal, the worldly man, is the man who has lost his faith; and the loss of perfect faith is the beginning of the end of the order erected upon that faith. Those who seek to preserve the prestige of truth without believing in it offer the most potent weapon to all their enemies; a merely metaphorical faith is suicidal. The radical attacks the Liberal doctrine at every point, and the veil of rhetoric is no protection against the strong thrust of his sharp blade. The Liberal, under this persistent attack, gives way on point after point, forced to admit the truth of the charges against him without being able to counter this negative, critical truth with any positive truth of his own; until, after a long and usually gradual transition, of a sudden he awakens to discover that the Old Order, undefended and seemingly indefensible, has been overthrown, and that a new, more "realistic"—and more brutal—truth has taken the field.

Liberalism is the first stage of the Nihilist dialectic, both because its own faith is empty, and because this emptiness calls into being a yet more Nihilist reaction—a reaction that, ironically, proclaims even more loudly than Liberalism its "love of truth," while carrying mankind one step farther on the path of error. This reaction is the second stage of the Nihilist dialectic: Realism.

2. REALISM

The Realism of which we speak—a generic term which we understand as inclusive of the various forms of "naturalism" and "positivism"—is, in its simplest form, the doctrine that was popularized precisely under the name of "Nihilism" by Turgenev in *Fathers and Sons*. The figure of Bazarov in that novel is the type of the "new man" of the 'sixties' in Russia, simple-minded materialists and determinists, who seriously thought (like D. Pisarev) to find the salvation of mankind in the dissection of the frog, or thought they had proved the non-existence of the human soul by failing to find it in the course of an autopsy. (One is reminded of the Soviet Nihilists, the "new men" of our own 'sixties,' who fail to find God in outer space.) This "Nihilist" is the man who respects nothing, bows before no authority, accepts (so he thinks) nothing on faith, judges all in the light of a science taken as absolute and exclusive truth, rejects all idealism and abstraction in favor of the concrete and factual. He is the believer, in a word, in the "nothing-but," in the reduction of everything men have considered "higher," the things of the mind and spirit, to the lower or "basic": matter, sensation, the physical.

As opposed to Liberal vagueness, the Realist world-view seems perfectly clear and straightforward. In place of agnosticism or an evasive deism, there is open atheism; in place of vague "higher values," naked materialism and self-interest. All is clarity in the Realist universe—except what is most important and most requires clarity: its beginning and end. Where the Liberal is vague about ultimate things, the Realist is childishly naive: they simply do not exist for him; nothing exists but what is most obvious.

Such Realism, of course, is a self-contradiction, whether it takes the form of a "naturalism" that tries to establish an absolute materialism and determinism, or a "positivism" that purports to deny the absolute altogether, or the doctrinaire "agnosticism" that so readily discourses on the "unknowability" of ultimate reality; we have already discussed this problem in Section I of this chapter. But argument, of course, is purely academic in view of the fact that Realism, a logical self-contradiction, is not properly treated as a philosophy at all. It is the naive, undisciplined thought of the unreflective, practical man who, in our age of oversimplification, thinks to impose his simple-minded standards and ideas upon the entire world; or, on a slightly different level, the equally naive thought of the scientist, bound to the obvious by the requirements of his specialty, when he illegitimately attempts to extend scientific criteria beyond their proper bounds. In the latter sense it is, to adopt a useful distinction,* "scientism" as opposed to legitimate science; for it must be understood that our remarks here are not directed against science itself, but against the improper exploitation of its standards and methods that is so common today.

Is it correct to call such a philosophy Nihilism? More precisely, is it Nihilism in the sense in which we have defined that term? If truth is, in the highest sense, knowledge of the beginning and end of things, of the dimension of the absolute; and if Nihilism is the doctrine that there is no such truth; then it is clear that those who take scientific knowledge for the only truth, and deny what lies above it, are Nihilists in the exact sense of that term. Worship of the fact is by no means the love of truth; it is, as we have already suggested, its parody. It is the presumption of the fragment to replace the whole; it is the proud attempt to build a Tower of Babel, a collection of facts, to reach to the heights of truth and wisdom from below. But truth is only attained by bowing down and accepting what is received from above. All the pretended "humility" of Realist scholars and scientists, these men of little faith, cannot conceal the pride of their collective usurpation of the throne of God; they, in

---

* A distinction made, for example, by Arnold Lunn in *The Revolt Against Reason,* New York, Sheed and Ward, 1951, p. 5 *et passim;* and by F. A. Hayek, in *The Counter-Revolution of Science,* Glencoe, Illinois, The Free Press, 1952, pp. 15–16. The former author is more concerned with theoretical, and the latter more with practical, "scientism."

their smallness, think their painstaking "research" of more weight than Divine Revelation. For such men, too, "there is no truth"; and of them we may say what St. Basil the Great said of pagan Greek scientists, "Their terrible condemnation will be the greater for all this worldly wisdom, since, seeing so clearly into vain sciences, they have willfully shut their eyes to the knowledge of the truth."*

Up to this point, however, we have failed properly to distinguish the second stage of Nihilism from its first. Most Liberals, too, accept science as exclusive truth; wherein does the Realist differ from them? The difference is not so much one of doctrine—Realism is in a sense merely disillusioned and systematized Liberalism—as one of emphasis and motivation. The Liberal is indifferent to absolute truth, an attitude resulting from excessive attachment to this world; with the Realist, on the other hand, indifference to truth becomes hostility, and mere attachment to the world becomes fanatical devotion to it. Those extreme consequences must have a more acute cause.

The Realist himself would say that this cause is the love of truth itself, which forbids belief in a "higher truth" that is no more than fantasy. Nietzsche, in fact, while believing this, saw in it a Christian quality that had turned against Christianity. "The sense of truth, highly developed through Christianity, ultimately revolts against the falsehood and fictitiousness of all Christian interpretations of the world and its history."** Understood in proper context, there is an insight—though partial and distorted—in these words. Nietzsche, most immediately, was rebelling against a Christianity that had been considerably diluted by Liberal humanism, a Christianity in which uncompromising love of and loyalty to absolute truth were rare if not entirely absent, a Christianity which had become no more than a moral idealism tinged with aesthetic sentiment. The Russian "Nihilists," similarly, were in revolt against the romantic idealism of "superfluous men" who dwelled in a nebulous realm of fantasy and escape divorced from any kind of reality, spiritual or worldly.

* *Hexaemeron,* I, 4.
** *The Will to Power,* p. 5.

Christian Truth is as remote from such pseudo-spirituality as is Nihilist realism. Both Christian and Realist are possessed of a love of truth, a will not to be deceived, a passion for getting to the root of things and finding their ultimate cause; both reject as unsatisfying any argument that does not refer to some absolute that itself needs no justification; both are the passionate enemies of the frivolity of a Liberalism that refuses to take ultimate things seriously and will not see human life as the solemn undertaking that it is. It is precisely this love of truth that will frustrate the attempt of Liberals to preserve ideas and institutions in which they do not fully believe, and which have no foundation in absolute truth. What is truth?—to the person for whom this is a vital, burning question, the compromise of Liberalism and humanism becomes impossible; he who once and with his whole being has asked this question can never again be satisfied with what the world is content to take in place of truth.

But it is not enough to ask this question; one must find the answer, or the last state of the seeker will be worse than the first. The Christian has found the only answer in God and His Son; the Realist, out of contact with Christian life and the Truth that animates it, asks the question in a spiritual vacuum and is content to accept the first answer he finds. Mistaking Christianity for another form of idealism, he rejects it and becomes a fanatical devotee of the only reality that is obvious to the spiritually blind: this world. Now, much as it is possible to admire the earnestness of the devoted materialist and atheist, not even the greatest charity can induce us to recognize in him any longer the love of truth which, perhaps, first inspired him; he is the victim, rather, of a love of truth that has gone astray, become a disease, and ended in its own negation. The motives of the Realist are, in fact, not pure: he claims to know what, by his own theory of knowledge, cannot be known (we have seen that the denial of absolute truth is itself an "absolute"); and if he does so it is because he has an ulterior motive, because he places some other worldly value above truth. The ruthless Realist and "truth-seeker" Nietzsche, seduced by a vision of the "Superman," ends in the evocation of the will to untruth and the will to power; Marxist Realism, for the sake of a revolutionary millennium, issues in a reign of lies and deceptions such as the world has never seen. The love of truth, frustrated of its proper object, is prostituted to an irrational "cause" and becomes a principle of subversion and destruction; it becomes the enemy of the truth it has failed to attain, of every kind of order founded wholly or partially upon the truth, and—in the end—of itself.

It becomes, in fact, a perfect parody of the Christian love of truth. Where the Christian asks the ultimate meaning of everything and is not content until he sees that it is founded on God and His Will, the Realist likewise questions everything, but only to be able to abolish all suggestion of or aspiration to anything higher, and to reduce and simplify it into the terms of the most obvious and "basic" explanation. Where the Christian sees God in everything, the Realist sees only "race" or "sex" or the "mode of production."

If the Realist, therefore, shares in common with the Christian a single-mindedness and earnestness that is totally foreign to the Liberal mentality, it is only the better to join in the Liberal's attack on Christian Truth, and to carry out that attack to its conclusion: the total abolition of Christian Truth. What began half-heartedly in Liberalism has gathered momentum in Realism and now presses to its catastrophic end. Nietzsche foresaw in our century "the triumph of Nihilism"; Jacob Burkhardt, that disillusioned Liberal, saw in it the advent of an age of dictators who would be *terribles simplificateurs.*" In Lenin and Stalin, Hitler and Mussolini, with their radically "simple" solutions for the most complex of problems, the fulfillment of this prediction in the political realm has been well begun. More profoundly, Nihilist "simplification" may be seen in the universal prestige today accorded the lowest order of knowledge, the scientific, as well as the simplistic ideas of men like Marx, Freud, and Darwin, which underlie virtually the whole of contemporary thought and life.

We say "life," for it is important to see that the Nihilist history of our century has not been something imposed from without or above, or at least has not been predominantly this; it has rather presupposed, and drawn its nourishment from, a Nihilist soil that has long been preparing in the hearts of the people. It is precisely from the Nihilism of the commonplace, from the everyday Nihilism revealed in the life and thought and aspiration of the people, that all the terrible events of our century have sprung. The world-view of Hitler is very instructive in this regard, for in him the most extreme and monstrous Nihilism rested upon the foundation of a quite unexceptional and even typical Realism. He shared the common faith in "science," "progress," and "enlightenment" (though not, of course, in "democracy"), together with a practical materialism that scorned all theology, metaphysics, and any thought or action concerned with any other world than the "here and now," priding himself on the fact that he had "the gift of reducing all problems to their simplest foundations."* He had a crude worship of efficiency and utility that freely tolerated "birth control," laughed at the institution of marriage as a mere legalization of a sexual impulse that should be "free," welcomed sterilization of the "unfit," despised "unproductive elements" such as monks, saw nothing in the cremation of the dead but a "practical" question and did not even hesitate to put the ashes, or the skin and fat, of the dead to "productive use." He possessed the quasi-anarchist distrust of sacred and venerable institutions, in particular the Church with its "superstitions" and all its "outmoded" laws and ceremonies. (We have already had occasion to note his abhorrence of the institution of Monarchy, a determining factor in his refusal to assume the Imperial title.) He had a naive trust in the "natural man," the "healthy animal" who scorns the Christian virtues—virginity in particular—that impede the "natural functioning" of the body. He took a simple-minded delight in modern conveniences and machines, and

---

* Quoted in Hermann Rauschning, *The Voice of Destruction,* New York, G. P. Putnam's Sons, 1940, p. 6. The rest of this description is based mainly on *Hitler's Secret Conversations, 1941–1944,* New York, Farrar, Straus and Young, 1953.

especially in the automobile and the sense of speed and "freedom" it affords.

There is very little of this crude *Weltanschauung* that is not shared, to some degree, by the multitudes today, especially among the young, who feel themselves "enlightened" and "liberated," very little that is not typically "modern." And it is precisely upon the basis of a Realism such as this, in which there is no more room for the "complicated" Christian view of life and the supremely important realities of the spiritual world, that the grossest superstitions and the most blatant credulity can thrive. Well-meaning men think to forestall the appearance of another Hitler by an attack upon "irrationality" and a defense of "reason," "science," and "common sense"; but outside of the context of Christian Truth these values, constituting a Realism of their own, are a preparation for, and not a defense against, the advent of another "terrible simplifier." The most effective contemporary "simplifiers" are those who hold power in the Soviet Union, who have made a religion of "science" and "common sense"; and anyone who looks to those most superstitious men for the defense of any value worth defending, is sorely deceived.

Realism unquestionably belongs to the "spirit of the age," and all who feel themselves to be of that "spirit" have had to accommodate themselves to it. Thus humanism, which in a more leisurely age had a more "idealistic" and Liberal coloration, has itself found it necessary to "change with the times" and adopt a more Realistic tone. The more naive have founded a humanistic "religion" that identifies itself with the cause of "science" and "progress" and has made into dogmas precisely the self-contradictions we have already examined;* it is men like this who are capable of seeing in Marxism too a kind of "humanism." But even in the most sophisticated of contemporary humanists, in the most urbane scholars and statesmen, the Realist tone is unmistakable. It is revealed, for example, in the invasion by scientific methods and attitudes of the last strongholds of the "humanities"; no contemporary

---

* See, for example, the writings of Corliss Lamont or Julian Huxley.

scholar, in whatever field, feels secure unless his work is to the fullest possible degree "scientific" (which often means, of course, "scientistic"). Realism may be seen, again, in the stoical, worldly-wise, and often cynical tone of all but the most naive (or religious) of contemporary humanists; their imagined "freedom from illusion" has also been, in large measure, a disillusionment; they now "know better" than to believe in the "higher truths" that comforted their fathers.

Humanism, in short, has come to terms with Realism—and, so it thinks, with reality; in the passage from Liberalism to Realism the humanist sees not only a disillusionment, but a process of "maturing." The Orthodox Christian, of course, sees something quite different. If the function of Liberalism was to obscure, with the smoke of "tolerance" and agnosticism, the higher truths concerning God and the spiritual life, the task of the Realism we have been examining has been to annihilate those truths. In this second stage in the progress of the Nihilist dialectic, Heaven has been closed off from the gaze of men, and men have resolved never again to take their eyes off the earth, but to live henceforth in and for this world alone. This Realist resolve is as present in a seemingly innocent "logical positivism" and scientific humanism as it is in the obviously Satanic phenomena of Bolshevism and National Socialism. The consequences of this resolve are hidden from those who make it, for they involve the very reality to which Realism is blind: the reality both above and below the narrow Realist universe. We shall see how the closing off of Heaven looses unexpected forces from below that make a nightmare of the Nihilist dream of a "new earth," and how the "new man" of Realism will resemble less a mythological "fully-developed" perfect humanity than a veritable "subhumanity" such as has never before been encountered in human experience.

We must now explore the next step in the progress of the Nihilism that leads to these ends: Vitalism.

3. VITALISM

Liberalism and Realism have been leading men, for a century and more, down a false path whose end, if the path had not been deflected, would have been something like one of those "reverse utopias" of which we have now heard so much,—a more terrible "brave new world," perhaps, an inhuman technological system wherein all worldly problems would be solved at the cost of the enslavement of men's souls. Against this utopia of rationalist planning many protests have been raised in the name of the concrete and personal, of the unplanned and unsystematic needs of human nature that are at least as essential, even for a purely worldly "happiness," as the more obvious material needs; a protest, above all, in the name of "life," which, whatever it may mean, would clearly be stifled in the Realist paradise.

The chief intellectual impetus of the Vitalist movement has been a reaction against the eclipse of higher realities in the Realist "simplification" of the world. This granted, we must on the other hand acknowledge the absolute failure of Vitalism on this level. Lacking sufficient foundation in or even awareness of Christian Truth, those who have applied themselves to the correction of the radical defects of Realism have generally invented remedies for them which have not been merely powerless, but positively harmful, remedies which are actually symptoms of a more advanced stage of the disease they were intended to heal.

For just as Realism, while reacting against the vagueness of Liberalism, condemned itself to sterility by accepting the Liberalist obscuration of higher truths, so too did Vitalism undermine its own hopes by accepting as an essential presupposition the critique of absolute truth made by the Realism it was attempting to combat. However much the Vitalist may yearn for the "spiritual" and "mystical," he will never look to Christian Truth for them, for that has been "outmoded" for him as surely as for the blindest Realist. Typical of the Vitalist attitude in this regard is the lament of W. B. Yeats in his autobiography over "being deprived by Huxley and Tyndall, whom I detested, of the simple-minded religion of my childhood...." Whatever psychological justification such an attitude may have, it has nothing whatever to do with the truth of things; and the consequences have been nothing but harmful. There is no form of Vitalism that is not naturalistic, none whose entire program does not begin and end in this world, none whose approach to any other world is anything but a parody. The path of Nihilism, let us note again, has been "progressive"; the errors of one of its stages are repeated and multiplied in its next stage.

There is no question, then, of finding in Vitalism a return to Christian—or any other—truths. There is, however, inevitably some pretense among Vitalists to do so. Many critics have noted the "pseudo-religious" character even of Marxism, though that epithet is applicable only to the misplaced fervor of its more enthusiastic devotees, and not to its doctrine, which is too clearly anti-religious in character. In Vitalism the question of "pseudo-religion" becomes much more serious. Here a quite understandable lament over the loss of spiritual values becomes father, on the one hand to subjective fantasies and (sometimes) to actual Satanism, which the undiscriminating take as revelations of the "spiritual" world, and on the other hand to a rootless eclecticism that draws ideas from every civilization and every age and finds a totally arbitrary connection between these misunderstood fragments and its own debased conceptions. Pseudo-spirituality and pseudo-traditionalism, one or both, are integral elements of many Vitalist systems. We must be cautious, then, in examining the claims of those who would restore a "spiritual" meaning to life, and especially of those who fancy themselves allies or adherents of "Christianity." "Spiritualist" errors are far more dangerous than any mere materialism; and we shall in fact find, in Part Three of this work, that most of what passes for "spirituality" today is in fact a "new spirituality," a cancer born of Nihilism that attaches itself to healthy organisms to destroy them from within. This tactic is the precise opposite of the bold Realist attack upon truth and the spiritual life; but it is no less a Nihilist tactic, and a more advanced one.

Intellectually, then, Vitalism presupposes a rejection of Christian Truth together with a certain pseudo-spiritual pretension. Realizing this, however, we shall still be unprepared to understand the Vitalist movement if we are unaware of the spiritual state of the men who have becomes its bearers. In Liberalism and Realism the Nihilist disease is still relatively superficial; it is still mainly a matter of philosophy and restricted to an intellectual elite. In Vitalism, however,—as already in Marxism, the most extreme manifestation of the Realist mentality—the disease not only develops qualitatively, it also extends itself quantitatively; for the first time the common people too begin to show signs of the Nihilism that was formerly restricted to the few.

This fact is, of course, in perfect accord with the internal logic of Nihilism, which aspires, like the Christianity it was called into existence to destroy, to universality. By the middle of the 19th century perceptive thinkers were expressing apprehension at the prospect of the "awakened" multitudes, those who were to be exploited by the "terrible simplifiers"; and by the time of Nietzsche, the most powerful of Vitalist "prophets," the apprehension had deepened and become a certainty. Nietzsche could see that the "death of God" had begun "to cast its first shadows over Europe"; and though "the event itself is far too great, too remote, too much beyond most people's power of apprehension, for one to suppose that so much as the report of it could have reached them," still its advent was certain, and it was men like Nietzsche who were "the firstlings and premature children of the coming century"*—the century, let us remember, of the "triumph of Nihilism."

The Christian Truth which Liberalism has undermined and Realism attacked is no mere philosophical Truth, but the Truth of life and salvation; and once there begins to gain ground, among the multitudes who have been nourished by that Truth, the conviction that it is no

---

* Friedrich Nietzsche, *The Joyful Wisdom,* #343.

longer credible, the result will be no mere urbane skepticism like that with which a few Liberals console themselves, but a spiritual catastrophe of enormous dimensions, one whose effect will make itself felt in every area of human life and thought. Thinkers like Nietzsche felt the presence of the first shadows of this catastrophe, and so were able to describe it in some detail and deduce certain of its consequences; but not until these shadows had begun to steal into the hearts of the multitudes could these consequences manifest themselves on a large scale. Toward the end of the nineteenth century increasing numbers of quite ordinary men had begun that restless search—so much a part of our own contemporary scenes—to find a substitute for the God Who was dead in their hearts. This restlessness has been the chief psychological impetus of Vitalism; it is raw material, as it were, ready to be shaped after the pattern of the intellectual presuppositions we have just examined, by craftsmen inspired by the latest current of the "spirit of the age." We tend, perhaps, to think of this restlessness mainly in terms of its exploitation by Nihilist demagogues, but it has been an important stimulant of Vitalist art and religion also. And the presence of this component in most Vitalist phenomena is the reason why they—as opposed to the seeming "sanity" of Liberalism and Realism—present symptoms, not merely of intellectual deviation, but of spiritual and psychological disorientation as well.

It will be well, before passing on to a consideration of the more formal manifestations of Vitalism in philosophy and art, to take a closer look at some of the common manifestations of this inarticulate restlessness that underlies them all. Is it as certain as we have implied that it is, after all, a Nihilist characteristic? Many will object that its significance has often been exaggerated, that it is simply a new form of something that has always existed, and that it is a ridiculous pretention to dignify something so common by the exalted name of Nihilism. There is, of course, some basis for such a judgment; nonetheless, it can hardly be denied that the modern phenomenon differs in several important respects from any of its predecessors. It exists today, for the first time in history, on a scale so vast as to be almost universal; "normal" remedies, the remedies of common sense, seem to have no effect whatever upon it, and if anything they seem to encourage it; and its course has exactly parallelled that of the extension of modern unbelief, so that if the one is not the cause of the other they are both at least parallel manifestations of one and the same process. These three points are so closely bound together that we shall not separate them in the following discussion, but examine them together.

The Fascist and National Socialist regimes were the most skillful in exploiting popular restlessness and utilizing it for their own purposes. But it is the "strange" fact—"strange" to anyone who does not understand the character of the age—that this restlessness has not been quieted by the defeat of its principal exploiters but has rather increased in intensity since then and—"strangest" of all—especially in the countries most advanced in the democratic and Liberal ideologies and most blessed with worldly prosperity, and in "backward" countries in direct proportion to their own progress toward these goals. Neither war nor Liberal idealism nor prosperity can pacify it—nor Marxist idealism either, for Soviet prosperity has produced the same phenomenon; these remedies are ineffective, for the disease lies deeper than they can reach.

Perhaps the most striking manifestation of the popular unrest has been in crime, and particularly in juvenile crime. Crime in most previous ages had been a localized phenomenon and had apparent and comprehensible causes in the human passions of greed, lust, envy, jealousy, and the like; never has there been anything more than a faint prefiguration of the crime that has become typical of our own century, crime for which the only name is one the avant-garde today is fond of using in another Nihilist context: "absurd."

A parent is murdered by a child, or a child by a parent; a total stranger is beaten or murdered—but not robbed—by an individual or a "gang"; such "gangs" terrorize whole neighborhoods by their prowling or their senseless wars with each other: and to what purpose? It is a time of "peace" and "prosperity," the criminals are as likely to be from the "best" as from the "worst" elements of society, there is no "practical" reason for their conduct and there is often complete disregard for precautions or consequences. When questioned, those apprehended for such crimes explain their behavior in the same way: it was an "impulse" or an "urge" that drove them, or there was a sadistic pleasure in committing the crime, or there was some totally irrelevant pretext, such as boredom, confusion, or resentment. In a word, they cannot explain their behavior at all, there is no readily comprehensible motive for it, and in consequence—and this is perhaps the most consistent and striking feature of such crimes—there is no remorse.

There are, of course, other less violent forms of the popular unrest. There is the passion for movement and speed, expressed especially in the veritable cult of the automobile (we have already noted this passion in Hitler); the universal appeal of television and cinema, whose most frequent function is to provide a few hours of escape from reality, both by their eclectic and "exciting" subject-matter and by the hypnotic effect of the media themselves; the increasingly primitive and savage character of popular music and of the perhaps more authentic expression of the contemporary soul, "jazz"; the cult of physical prowess in sport, and the morbid worship of "youth" of which it is a part; the prevalence of and general permissiveness towards sexual promiscuity, condoned by many supposedly responsible elders as indicative of the "frankness" of contemporary youth and as being merely another form of the "open," "experimental" attitude so much encouraged in the arts and sciences; the disrespect for authority fostered by a popular attitude that sees no values but the "immediate" and "dynamic" and leads the most "idealistic" of youth into demonstrations against "repressive" laws and institutions.

In such phenomena "activity" is clearly an escape—an escape from boredom, from meaninglessness, and most profoundly from the emptiness that takes possession of the heart that has abandoned God, Revealed Truth, and the morality and conscience dependent upon that

Truth. In the more complex manifestations of the Vitalist impulse, to which we now turn, the same psychology is at work. We shall do no more than suggest the wealth of these manifestations, for we shall examine most of them in some detail later in their role as forms of the "new spirituality."

In politics, the most successful forms of Vitalism have been Mussolini's cult of activism and violence, and Hitler's darker cult of "blood and soil"; the nature of these is too familiar to the present generation to need further comment in this context. It is perhaps not so obvious today, however, when the political barometer so clearly points to the "left," just how profound was the appeal of these movements when they appeared some forty years ago. Quite apart from the uprooted masses, who were the principle object of their exploitation, a not inconsiderable section of the intellectual and cultural avant-garde also became enthusiastic sympathizers of the Nihilist demagogues, at least for a while. If few among the sophisticated took either Naziism or Fascism as a "new religion," some at least welcomed one or the other of them as a salutary antidote to the "democracy," "science," and "progress" (that is, the Liberalism and Realism) that seemed to promise a future no sensitive man could envision without apprehension; their "dynamism," "vitality," and pseudo-traditionalism seemed deceptively "refreshing" to many who were breathing the stifling intellectual atmosphere of the time.

Modern art has had a similar appeal, and its similar reaction against lifeless academic "realism" has likewise led into strange fields. New and exotic sources and influences have been found in the art of Africa, the Orient, the South Seas, of prehistoric man, children, and madmen, in spiritism and occultism. Continual "experimentation" has been the rule, a constant search for "new" forms and techniques; inspiration has been found above all in the "savage," the "primitive," and the "spontaneous." Like the Futurists in their manifesto (though Futurism itself can hardly be taken seriously as art), the most typical modern artists have exalted in their works "every kind of originality, boldness, extreme violence," and they have likewise believed that "our hands are free and pure, to start everything afresh."

The artist, according to the Vitalist myth, is a "creator," a "genius," he is "inspired." In his art Realism is transformed by "vision"; it is a sign and a prophecy of a "spiritual awakening." The artist, in short, is a "magician" in his own realm in precisely the same way Hitler was in politics; and in both it is not truth, but subjective feeling, that reigns.

In religion—or, to speak more precisely, pseudo-religion—the restless experimentation characteristic of Vitalism has manifested itself in even more varied forms than it has in the schools of modern art. There are, for example, the sects whose deity is a vague, immanent "force"; these are the varieties of "new thought" and "positive thinking," whose concern is to harness and utilize this "force," as if it were a kind of electricity. Closely related to these are occultism and spiritism, as well as certain spurious forms of "Eastern wisdom," which abandon all pretense of concern with "God" explicitly to invoke more immediate "powers" and "presences."

Religious Vitalism appears also in the widespread cult of "awareness" and "realization." In a fairly restrained form this is present in the devotees of modern art and the "creative act" and "vision" that inspire this art. The indiscriminate quest for "enlightenment," as in those under the influence of Zen Buddhism, is a more extreme form of this cult; and the supposed "religious experience" stimulated by various drugs is, perhaps, its *reductio ad absurdum.*

Again, there is the attempt to fabricate a pseudo-pagan cult of "nature," and especially of its most "primary" and "basic" elements: the earth, the body, sex. Nietzsche's "Zarathustra" is a powerful "prophet" of this cult, and it is the central theme of D. H. Lawrence and other novelists and poets of this century.

And there is the attempt, in most kinds of "existentialism" and "personalism," to turn religion into no more than a personal "encounter" with other men and—sometimes—with a vaguely-conceived

"God"; or, in pathological, atheistic "existentialism," to make a religion of "rebellion" and frenzied self-worship.

All of these Vitalist manifestations of the "religious impulse" share in common a hostility to any stable or unchanging doctrine or institution and a paramount concern with and pursuit of the "immediate" values of "life," "vitality," "experience," "awareness," or "ecstasy."

We have delineated the most striking features of Vitalism and given some suggestion of its extent; but we have yet to define the term itself and expose its Nihilist character. Liberalism, as we have seen, undermined truth by indifference to it, retaining however the prestige of its name; and Realism attacked it in the name of a lesser, partial truth. Vitalism, as opposed to both of these, has no relation to truth whatever; it simply devotes its whole concern to something of an entirely different order.

"The falseness of an opinion," said Nietzsche, "is not for us any objection to it…. The question is, how far an opinion is life-furthering, life-preserving…."* When such pragmatism begins, Nihilism passes into the Vitalist stage, which may be defined as the elimination of truth as the criterion of human action, and the substitution of a new standard: the "life-giving," the "vital"; it is the final divorce of life from truth.

Vitalism is a more advanced kind of Realism; sharing the latter's narrow view of reality and its concern to reduce everything higher to the lowest possible terms, Vitalism carries the Realist intention one step further. Where Realism tries to reestablish an absolute truth from below, Vitalism expresses the failure of this project in the face of the more "realistic" awareness that there is no absolute here below, that the only unchanging principle in this world is change itself. Realism reduces the supernatural to the natural, the Revealed to the rational, truth to objectivity; Vitalism goes further and reduces everything to subjective experience and sensation. The world that seemed so solid, the truth that seemed so secure to the Realist, dissolve in the Vitalist view of things;

---

* Friedrich Nietzsche, *Beyond Good and Evil*, #4.

the mind has no more place to rest, everything is swallowed up in movement and action.

The logic of unbelief leads inexorably to the Abyss; he who will not return to the truth must follow error to its end. So does humanism, too, after having contracted the Realist infection, succumb to the Vitalist germ. Of this fact there is no better indication than the "dynamic" standards that have come to occupy an increasingly large place in formal criticism of art and literature, and even in discussions of religion, philosophy, and science. There are no qualities more prized in any of these fields today than those of being "original," "experimental," or "exciting"; the question of truth, if it is raised at all, is more and more forced into the background and replaced by subjective criteria: "integrity," "authenticity," "individuality."

Such an approach is an open invitation to obscurantism, not to mention charlatanry; and if the latter may be dismissed as a temptation for the Vitalist that has not become the rule, it is by no means possible to ignore the increasingly blatant obscurantism which the Vitalist temperament tolerates and even encourages. It becomes ever more difficult in the contemporary intellectual climate to engage in rational discussion with Vitalist apologists. If one, for example, inquires into the meaning of a contemporary work of art, he will be told that it has no "meaning," that it is "pure art" and can only be "felt," and that if the critic does not "feel" it properly he has no right to comment on it. The attempt to introduce any standard of criticism, even of the most elementary and technical sort, is countered by the claim that old standards cannot be applied to the new art, that they are "static," "dogmatic," or simply "out-of-date," and that art today can be judged only in terms of its success in fulfilling its own unique intentions. If the critic sees a morbid or inhuman intent behind a work of art, the apology is that it is an accurate reflection of the "spirit of the age," and it is implied that a man is naive if he believes that art should be more than that. The latter argument is, of course, the favorite one of every avant-garde today, whether literary, philosophical, or "religious." For men weary of truth it is enough that a thing "is," and that it is "new" and "exciting."

These are, perhaps, understandable reactions to the overly literary and utilitarian approach of Liberalism and Realism to realms like art and religion which use a language quite unlike the prosaic language of science and business; to criticize them effectively, surely, one must understand their language and know what it is they are trying to say. But what is equally clear is that *they are trying to say something:* everything man does has a meaning, and every serious artist and thinker is trying to communicate something in his work. If it be proclaimed there is no meaning, or that there is only the desire to express the "spirit of the age," or that there is no desire to communicate at all—why, these too are meanings, and very ominous ones, which the competent critic will surely notice. Unfortunately, but very significantly, the task of criticism today has been virtually identified with that of apology; the role of the critic is generally seen to be no more than that of explaining, for the uninstructed multitudes, the latest "inspiration" of the "creative genius."* Thus passive "receptivity" takes the place of active intelligence, and "success"—the success of the "genius" in expressing his intention, no matter what the nature of that intention—replaces excellence. By the new standards Hitler too was "successful," until the "spirit of the age" proved him "wrong"; and the avant-garde and its humanist "fellow-travellers" have no argument whatever against Bolshevism today, unless it be that, unlike National Socialism, which was "expressionistic" and "exciting," it is completely prosaic and Realistic.

But perhaps most revealing of the infection of humanism by Vitalism is the strange axiom, romantic and skeptical at the same time, that the "love of truth" is never-ending because it can never be fulfilled, that the whole of life is a constant search for something there is no hope of finding, a constant movement that never can—nor should—know a

---

* Some cogent remarks on this and related topics, with reference to modern literature, are to be found in Graham Hough, *Reflections on a Literary Revolution,* Washington, The Catholic University of America Press, 1960, p. 66ff.

place of rest. The sophisticated humanist can be very eloquent in describing this, the new first principle of scholarly and scientific research, as an acknowledgement of the "provisional" nature of all knowledge, as a reflection of the never-satisfied, ever-curious human mind, or as part of the mysterious process of "evolution" or "progress"; but the significance of the attitude is clear. It is the last attempt of the unbeliever to hide his abandonment of truth behind a cloud of noble rhetoric, and, more positively, it is at the same time the exaltation of petty curiosity to the place once occupied by the genuine love of truth. Now it is quite true to say that curiosity, exactly like its analogue, lust, never ends and is never satisfied; but man was made for something more than this. He was made to rise, above curiosity and lust, to love, and through love to the attainment of truth. This is an elementary truth of human nature, and it requires, perhaps, a certain simplicity to grasp it. The intellectual trifling of contemporary humanism is as far from such simplicity as it is from truth.

The appeal of Vitalism is, as we have already suggested, quite understandable psychologically. Only the dullest and least perceptive of men can remain satisfied for long with the dead faith of Liberalism and Realism. Extreme elements first—artists, revolutionaries, the uprooted multitudes—and then, one by one, the humanist guardians of "civilization," and eventually even the most respectable and conservative elements of society, become possessed of an inner disquiet that leads them into the pursuit of something "new" and "exciting," no one knows exactly what. Nihilist prophets, at first generally scorned, come into fashion as men come to share their unrest and forebodings; they are gradually incorporated into the humanist pantheon and are looked to for insights and revelations that will take men out of the barren desert into which Realism has led them. Beneath the trivial sensationalism and eclecticism that characterize the contemporary trend to "mysticism" and "spiritual values," lies a deep hunger for something more substantial than Liberalism and Realism have provided or can provide, a hunger that the varieties of Vitalism can only tease, but never satisfy.

Men have rejected the Son of God Who, even now, desires to dwell in men and bring them salvation; and finding intolerable the vacuum this rejection has left in their hearts, they run to madmen and magicians, to false prophets and religious sophists, for a word of life. But this word, so readily given, itself turns to dust in their mouths when they try to repeat it.

Realism, in its rage for truth, destroys the truth; in the same way Vitalism, in its very quest for life, smells of death. The Vitalism of the last hundred years has been an unmistakable symptom of world-weariness, and its prophets—even more clearly than any of the philosophers of the dead Liberalism and Realism they attacked—have been a manifestation of the end of Christian Europe. Vitalism is the product, not of the "freshness" and "life" and "immediacy" its followers so desperately seek (precisely because they lack them), but of the corruption and unbelief that are but the last phase of the dying civilization they hate. One need be no partisan of the Liberalism and Realism against which Vitalism reacted to see that it has "over-reacted," that its antidote to an undeniable disease is itself a more potent injection of the same Nihilist germ that caused the disease. Beyond Vitalism there can be only one more, definitive, stage through which Nihilism may pass: the Nihilism of Destruction.

4. THE NIHILISM OF DESTRUCTION

Here at last we find an almost "pure" Nihilism, a rage against creation and against civilization that will not be appeased until it has reduced them to absolute nothingness. The Nihilism of Destruction, if no other form of Nihilism, is unique to the modern age. There has been destruction on a wide scale before, and there have been men who have gloried in destruction; but never until our own time have there been a doctrine and a plan of destruction, never before has the mind of man so contorted itself as to find an apology for this most obvious work of Satan, and to set up a program for its accomplishment.

Even among more restrained Nihilists, to be sure, there have been strong intimations of the gospel of destruction. The Realist Bazarov could state that "there is not a single institution of our society that should not be destroyed."* "Who wishes to be creative," said Nietzsche, "must first destroy and smash accepted values." The Manifesto of the Futurists—who were perhaps as near to pure Nihilism as to Vitalism—glorified war and "the destroying arm of the anarchist." The destruction of the Old Order and the abolition of absolute truth were the admitted aims of most Realists and Vitalists.

In the pure Nihilists, however, what to others was prologue becomes an end in itself. Nietzsche proclaimed the basic principle of all Nihilism, and the special apology of the Nihilism of Destruction, in the phrase, "There is no truth, all is permitted";** but the extreme consequences of this axiom had already been realized before him. Max Stirner (whom we shall encounter again in the next chapter)*** declared war upon every standard and every principle, proclaiming his ego against the world and laughing triumphantly over the "tomb of humanity"—all, as yet, in theory. Sergei Nechayev translated this theory into practice so perfectly that to this day he seems a creation of myth, if not a demon from the depths of Hell itself, leading a life of unprincipled ruthlessness and amorality, under the pretext of total expediency in the name of the Revolution. He was the inspiration for the character of Pyotr Verkhovensky in *The Possessed* of Dostoyevsky, a novel so brilliant in its characterization of the extreme Nihilist mentality (the book in fact is full of representatives of this mentality) as to be absolutely incredible to anyone who has not, like Dostoyevsky, himself known the fascination and temptation of Nihilism.

Michael Bakunin, who fell under the spell of Nechayev for a while, only to discover that the consistent practice of Nihilism was a

* Ivan S. Turgenev, *Fathers and Sons.*
** Quoted in Karl Jaspers, *Nietzsche and Christianity,* Henry Regnery Company, 1961 (Gateway Edition), p. 83.
*** The next chapter was to be on Anarchism (see outline below, p. 100).—Ed.

quite different thing from its theoretical exposition, wrote under this spell a "Revolutionary Catechism" that provided a chilling apology for Nechayevism while proclaiming, "our task is terrible, total, inexorable, and universal destruction." The sentiment is too typical of Bakunin to be explained away by his momentary fascination. He ended his *Reaction in Germany,* written before Nechayev was born, with the famous appeal, "Let us put our trust in the eternal spirit which destroys and annihilates only because it is the unsearchable and eternally creative source of all life. The passion for destruction is also a creative passion!" Here Vitalism mingles with the will to destroy: but it is destruction that triumphs in the end. Asked what he would do if the new order of his dreams should come into existence, he frankly replied, "Then I should at once begin to pull down again everything I had made."*

It was in the spirit of Nechayev and the "Revolutionary Catechism" that Nihilist assassins (they were called at the time "anarchist," but we have adopted the more positive meaning of that word in this book), with their "propaganda of the deed," terrorized the ruling classes—and not only the ruling classes—in Europe and especially in Russia throughout the last quarter of the 19th century. It was in the same spirit that Lenin (who greatly admired Nechayev) assumed ruthless power and began Europe's first successful experiment in totally unprincipled politics. The passion for violence, divorced from the Revolution which rationalized it, helped lead Europe into the first of its Nihilist wars in 1914, and at the same time, in another realm, announced in Dadaist art, "let everything be swept away," "no more of anything, *nothing, nothing, nothing.*" It remained, however, for Hitler to reveal with absolute explicitness the nature and ends of a pure "Revolution of Nihilism," a revolution committed to the equally Nihilist alternatives of *Weltmacht oder Niedergang:* world-conquest or total ruin; a Revolution whose Leader could exult (even before he had come to power), even as Stirner would have exulted, that "we may be

* Quoted in E. H. Carr, *Michael Bakunin,* p. 440.

destroyed, but if we are, we shall drag a world with us—a world in flames."*

Such phenomena, of course, are extreme, and they must be viewed in proper perspective. Only a few have been capable of such pure Nihilism, and it could easily be argued that they do not belong to the main stream of modern history, but to a side current; and less extreme Nihilists condemn them. Their example has been, nonetheless, a most instructive one, and it would be a mistake to dismiss this example as mere exaggeration or parody. We shall see that destruction is an indispensable item in the program of Nihilism, and further that it is the most unequivocal expression of the worship of Nothingness that lies at the center of the Nihilist "theology." The Nihilism of Destruction is not an exaggeration, it is rather a fulfillment of the deepest aim of all Nihilism. In it Nihilism has assumed its most terrible, but its truest form; in it the face of Nothingness discards its masks and stands revealed in all its nakedness.

Father John of Kronstadt, that holy man of God, has likened the soul of man to an eye, diseased through sin and thus incapable of seeing the spiritual sun.** The same likeness may serve to trace the progress of the disease of Nihilism, which is no more than an elaborate mask of sin. The spiritual eye in fallen human nature is not sound, as every Orthodox Christian knows; we see in this life only dimly and require faith and the Grace of God to effect a healing that will enable us, in the future life, to see clearly once more. The first stage of Nihilism, which is Liberalism, is born of the errors of taking our diseased eye for a sound one, of mistaking its impaired vision for a view of the true world, and thus of discharging the physician of the soul, the Church, whose ministrations are not needed by a "healthy" man. In the second stage, Realism, the disease, no longer attended by the necessary physician, begins to grow; vision is narrowed; distant objects, already ob-

* Quoted in Rauschning, *op. cit.,* p. 5.
** *My Life in Christ,* Jordanville, New York, Holy Trinity Monastery, 1957, Vol. I., p. 178.

scure enough in the "natural" state of impaired vision, become invisible; only the nearest objects are seen distinctly, and the patient becomes convinced no others exist. In the third stage, Vitalism, infection leads to inflammation; even the nearest objects become dim and distorted and there are hallucinations. In the fourth stage, the Nihilism of Destruction, blindness ensues and the disease spreads to the rest of the body, effecting agony, convulsions, and death.

III.

The Theology and the Spirit of Nihilism

1. REBELLION: THE WAR AGAINST GOD

OUR inquiry thus far has concentrated upon definition and description; if it has been successful, it has identified the Nihilist mentality and furnished some idea of its origins and extent. All this, however, has been but necessary groundwork for the task to which we must now turn: an exploration of the deeper me aning of Nihilism. Our earlier examination has been historical, psychological, philosophical; but the Revolution, as we saw in the last chapter,* has a theological and spiritual foundation, even if its "theology" is an inverted one and its "spirituality" Satanic. The Orthodox Christian finds in the Revolution a formidable antagonist, and one that must be fought, fairly and thoroughly, with the best weapons at his disposal. It is time, then, to attack the Nihilist doctrine at its root; to inquire into its theological sources, its spiritual roots, its ultimate program, and its role in the Christian theology of history.

Nihilist doctrine is not, of course, explicit in most Nihilists; and if our analysis to this point has had to draw out implications that were not always obvious to, and often not intended by, Nihilists themselves, our attempt here to extract a coherent doctrine from the literature and

---

* The previous chapter was to be on the Advent of the New Order (see outline below, p. 100).—ED.

phenomena of Nihilism will seem, to many, to carry us to yet more tenuous conclusions. In this task we are, however, greatly aided by systematic Nihilists like Nietzsche, who express unequivocally what others only suggest or attempt to disguise, and by acute observers of the Nihilist mentality like Dostoyevsky, whose insights strike to the very heart of Nihilism and strip aside its masks.

In no one has the Nihilist "revelation" been more clearly expressed than in Nietzsche. We have already seen this "revelation" in its philosophical form, in the phrase "there is no truth." Its alternative, more explicitly theological expression in Nietzsche is the constant theme, significantly, of the inspired "prophet," Zarathustra; and in its earliest occurrence in Nietzsche's writings it is the "ecstatic" utterance of a madman: "God is dead."* The words express a certain truth: not, to be sure, a truth of the nature of things, but a truth concerning the state of modern man; they are an imaginative attempt to describe a fact no Christian, surely, will deny.

God is dead in the hearts of modern man: this is what the "death of God" means, and it is as true of the atheists and Satanists who rejoice in the fact, as it is of the unsophisticated multitudes in whom the sense of the spiritual reality has simply disappeared. Man has lost faith in God and in the Divine Truth that once sustained him; the apostasy to worldliness that has characterized the modern age since its beginning becomes, in Nietzsche, conscious of itself and finds words to express itself. "God is dead": that is to say, "we have lost our faith in God"; "there is no truth": that is to say, "we have become uncertain of everything divine and absolute."

Deeper, however, than the subjective fact the Nihilist "revelation" expresses, lie a will and a plan that go far beyond any mere acceptance of "fact." Zarathustra is a "prophet"; his words are clearly intended as a counter-revolution directed against the Christian Revelation. For those, indeed, who accept the new "revelation"—i.e., for those who feel it to be

---

* *The Joyful Wisdom,* #125.

their own self-confession, or who live as though it were—an entirely new spiritual universe opens up, in which God exists no longer, in which, more significantly, men do not *wish* God to exist. Nietzsche's "madman" knows that men have "murdered" God, have killed their own faith.†

It is decidedly wrong, then, to regard the modern Nihilist, in whatever guise he may appear, as "agnostic." The "death of God" has not simply happened to him as a kind of cosmic catastrophe, rather he has actively *willed* it—not directly, to be sure, but equally effectively by preferring something else to the true God. Nor is the Nihilist, let us note, really atheistic. It may be doubted, indeed, if there exists such a thing as "atheism," for no one denies the true God except to devote himself to the service of a false god; the atheism that is possible to the philosopher (though it is, of course, bad philosophy) is not possible to the whole man. The Anarchist Proudhon (whose doctrine we shall examine more closely in the next chapter) saw this clearly enough, and declared himself, not an atheist, but an "antitheist";* "the Revolution is not atheistic, in the strict sense of the word … it does not deny the absolute, it eliminates it…."** "The first duty of man, on becoming intelligent and free, is to continually hunt the idea of God out of his mind and conscience. For God, if he exists, is essentially hostile to our nature…. Every step we take in advance is a victory in which we crush Divinity."*** Humanity must be made to see that "God, if there is a God, is its enemy."**** Albert Camus, in effect, teaches the same doctrine when he raises "rebellion" (and not "unbelief") to the rank of first principle. Bakunin, too, was not content to "refute" the existence of God; "If God really existed," he believed, "it would be necessary to abolish him."† More effectively, the Bolshevist "atheism" of our cen-

---

* See, for example, *Justice,* (cf. de Lubac, *Proudhon,* p. 271).
** *Justice,* III, 179. (Quoted de Lubac, p. 270.)
*** *System of Economical Contradictions: or, The Philosophy of Misery,* Boston, 1888, Vol. I, p. 448.
**** *Ibid.,* p. 468.
† *God and the State,* London, 1910, p. 16.

tury has been quite obviously a war to the death against God and all His works.

Revolutionary Nihilism stands irrevocably and explicitly against God; but philosophical and existentialist Nihilism—a fact not always so clear—is equally "antitheistic" in its assumption that modern life must henceforth continue without God. The army of the enemies of God is recruited as much from the many who passively accept their position in the rear guard as from the few active enthusiasts who occupy the front ranks. More important to observe, however, is the fact that the ranks of antitheism are swelled not only by active and passive "atheists," but by many who think themselves "religious" and worship some "god." Robespierre established a cult of the "Supreme Being," Hitler recognized the existence of a "supreme force," a "god within men," and all forms of Nihilist Vitalism have a "god" something like Hitler's. The war against God is capable of a variety of stratagems, among them the use of the name of God, and even of Christ. But whether it is explicitly "atheist," or "agnostic," or takes the form of a worship of some "new god," Nihilism has for its foundation the declaration of war against the true God.

Formal atheism is the philosophy of a fool (if we may so paraphrase the Psalmist);* but antitheism is a profounder malady. The literature of antitheism, to be sure, is as full of inconsistencies and contradictions as is formally atheist literature; but where the latter errs through childishness (and the most sophisticated man in one discipline can easily be a child in theology and the spiritual life) and through plain insensitivity to spiritual realities, the former owes its distortions to a deep-seated passion that, recognizing these realities, wills to destroy them. The petty arguments of Bertrand Russell (though even his atheism is, of course, ultimately a kind of antitheism) are easily explained and refuted, and they are no danger to a secure faith; but the profound and determined attack of

---

* Psalm LII (LIII), 1: "The fool hath said in his heart, there is no God."

Proudhon is a different matter, for it is born not of bloodless sophistry but of great fervor.

Here we must face squarely a fact at which we have hinted before now, but which we have not yet fully examined: Nihilism is animated by a faith as strong, in its own way, and as spiritual in its root, as the Christian faith it attempts to destroy and supplant; its success, and its exaggerations, are explicable in no other way.

We have seen Christian faith to be the spiritual context wherein the questions of God, Truth, and Authority become meaningful and inspire consent. Nihilist faith is similarly a context, a distinctive spirit which underlies and gives meaning and power to Nihilist doctrine. The success of Nihilism in our time has been dependent upon, and may be measured by, the spread of this spirit; its arguments seem persuasive not to the degree that they are true, but to the degree that this spirit has prepared men to accept them.

What, then, is the nature of the Nihilist faith? It is the precise opposite of Christian faith, and so not properly called "faith" at all. Where Christian faith is joyous, certain, serene, loving, humble, patient, submitting in all things to the Will of God, its Nihilist counterpart is full of doubt, suspicion, disgust, envy, jealousy, pride, impatience, rebelliousness, blasphemy—one or more of these qualities predominating in any given personality. It is an attitude of dissatisfaction with self, with the world, with society, with God; it knows but one thing: *that it will not accept things as they are,* but must devote its energies either to changing them or fleeing from them. It was well described by Bakunin as "the sentiment of rebellion, this Satanic pride, which spurns subjection to any master whatever, whether of divine or human origin."*

Nihilist rebellion, like Christian faith, is an ultimate and irreducible spiritual attitude, having its source and its strength in itself—and, of course, in the supernatural author of rebellion. We shall be unpre-

---

* Maximoff, *op. cit.,* p. 380.

pared to understand the nature or the success of Nihilism, or the existence of systematic representatives of it like Lenin and Hitler, if we seek its source anywhere but in the primal Satanic will to negation and rebellion. Most Nihilists, of course, understand this will as something positive, as the source of "independence" and "freedom"; but the very language in which men like Bakunin find it necessary to express themselves, betrays the deeper import of their words to anyone prepared to take them seriously.

The Nihilist rejection of Christian faith and institutions, then, is the result, not so much of a loss of faith in them and in their divine origin (though, no Nihilism being pure, this skepticism is present also), as of rebellion against the authority they represent and the obedience they command. The literature of 19th-century Humanism, Socialism, and Anarchism has as its constant theme the *non serviam:* God the Father, together with all His institutions and ministers, is to be overthrown and crushed, and triumphant Man is to ascend His throne to rule in his own right. This literature, intellectually mediocre, owes its power and its continuing influence to its "righteous" indignation against the "injustices" and "tyranny" of the Father and His earthly representatives; to its passion, that is, and not to its truth.

This rebellion, this messianic fervor that animates the greatest revolutionaries, being an inverse faith, is less concerned to demolish the philosophical and theological foundation of the Old Order (that task can be left to less fervent souls) than to destroy the rival faith which gave it life. Doctrines and institutions may be "reinterpreted," emptied of their Christian content and filled with a new, Nihilist content; but Christian faith, the soul of these doctrines and institutions and alone capable of discerning this "reinterpretation" and effectively opposing it, must be completely destroyed before it can itself be "reinterpreted." This is a practical necessity if Nihilism is to triumph; more, it is a psychological and even a spiritual necessity, for Nihilist rebellion dimly senses that the Truth resides in Christian faith, and its jealousy and its uneasy conscience will not be appeased until the total abolition of faith has justified its position and "proved" its truth. On a minor scale, this is the psychology of the Christian apostate; on a major scale, it is the psychology of Bolshevism.

The systematic Bolshevik campaign to uproot Christian faith, even when it has clearly ceased to be a danger to the stability of the atheist state, has no rational explanation; it is rather part of a ruthless war to the death against the only force capable of standing against Bolshevism and of "disproving" it. Nihilism has failed as long as true Christian faith remains in a single person; for that person will be a living example of Truth that will prove vain all the impressive worldly accomplishments of which Nihilism is capable and will refute in his person all the arguments against God and the Kingdom of Heaven. Man's mind is supple, and it can be made to believe anything to which his will inclines. In an atmosphere permeated with Nihilistic fervor, such as still exists in the Soviet Union, the soundest argument can do nothing to induce belief in God, in immortality, in faith; but a man of faith, even in this atmosphere, can speak to the heart of man and show, by his example, that what is impossible to the world and to the best of human intentions, is still possible to God and to faith.

Nihilist rebellion is a war against God and against Truth; but few Nihilists are fully aware of this. Explicit theological and philosophical Nihilism is the preserve of a few rare souls; for most, Nihilist rebellion takes the more immediate form of a war against authority. Many whose attitudes toward God and Truth may seem ambiguous reveal their Nihilism most clearly in their attitude toward—in Bakunin's words—the "cursed and fatal principle of authority."*

The Nihilist "revelation" thus declares, most immediately, the annihilation of authority. Some apologists are fond of citing "corruptions," "abuses," and "injustices" in the Old Order as justification for rebellion against it; but such things—the existence of which no one will deny—have been often the pretext, but never the cause, of Nihilist

---

* *Ibid.,* p. 253.

outbursts. It is authority itself that the Nihilist attacks. In the political and social order, Nihilism manifests itself as a Revolution that intends, not a mere change of government or a more or less widespread reform of the existing order, but the establishment of an entirely new conception of the end and means of government. In the religious order Nihilism seeks, not a mere reform of the Church and not even the foundation of a new "church" or "religion," but a complete refashioning of the idea of religion and of spiritual experience. In art and literature the Nihilist is not concerned with the modification of old aesthetic canons regarding subject-matter or style, nor with the development of new genres or traditions, but with a whole new approach to the question of artistic "creation" and a new definition of "art."

It is the very first principles of these disciplines, and no mere remote or faulty applications of them, that Nihilism attacks. The disorder so apparent in contemporary politics, religion, art, and other realms as well, is a result of the deliberate and systematic annihilation of the foundations of authority in them. Unprincipled politics and morality, undisciplined artistic expression, indiscriminate "religious experience"—all are the direct consequence of the application to once stable sciences and disciplines of the attitude of rebellion.

Nihilist rebellion has entered so deeply into the fibre of our age that resistance to it is feeble and ineffective; popular philosophy and most "serious thought" devote their energies to apology for it. Camus, in fact, sees in rebellion the only self-evident truth left to the men of today, the only belief remaining to men who can no longer believe in God. His philosophy of rebellion is a skillful articulation of the "spirit of the age," but it is hardly to be taken seriously as anything more than that. Thinkers of the Renaissance and the Enlightenment were as anxious as Camus is today to do without theology, to base all their knowledge on "nature." But if "rebellion" is all the "natural man" may know today, why is it that the "natural man" of the Renaissance or the Enlightenment seemed to know much more, and thought himself to be a much nobler being. "They took too much for granted," is the usual answer, "and lived on Christian capital without knowing it; today we are bankrupt, and know it." Contemporary man, in a word, is "disillusioned." But, strictly speaking, one must be "disillusioned" of an illusion: if men have fallen way, not from illusion, but from truth—and this is indeed the case—then profounder reasoning is required to explain their present "plight." That Camus can accept the "rebel" as the "natural man," that he can find everything "absurd" except "rebellion," means only one thing: he has been well-trained in the school of Nihilism, he has learned to accept the fight against God as the "natural" state of man.

To such a state has Nihilism reduced men. Before the modern age the life of man was largely conditioned by the virtues of obedience, submission, and respect: to God, to the Church, to the lawful earthly authorities. To the modern man whom Nihilism has "enlightened," this Old Order is but a horrible memory of some dark past from which man has been "liberated"; modern history has been the chronicle of the fall of every authority. The Old Order has been overthrown, and if a precarious stability is maintained in what is unmistakably an age of "transition," a "new order" is clearly in the making; the age of the "rebel" is at hand.

Of this age the Nihilist regimes of this century have given a foretaste, and the widespread rebelliousness of the present day is a further portent; where there is no truth, the rebellious will reigns. But "the will," said Dostoyevsky, with his customary insight into the Nihilist mentality, "is closest to nothing; the most assertive are closest to the most nihilistic."* He who has abandoned truth and every authority founded upon that truth has only blind will between himself and the Abyss; and this will, whatever its spectacular achievements in its brief moment of power (those of Hitler and of Bolshevism have so far been the most spectacular), is irresistibly drawn to that Abyss as to some immense magnet that has searched out the answering abyss within itself.

---

* Quoted by Robert Payne in *Zero,* New York, The John Day Company, 1950, p. 53.

In this abyss, this nothingness of the man who lives without truth, we come to the very heart of Nihilism.

2. THE WORSHIP OF NOTHINGNESS

"Nothingness," in the sense in which modern Nihilism understands it, is a concept unique to the Christian tradition. The "non-being" of various Eastern traditions is an entirely different, a positive, conception; the nearest they approach to the idea of *nihil* is their obscure notion of primal "chaos." God has spoken only obscurely and indirectly to other peoples; to His chosen people alone has He revealed the fullness of truth concerning the beginning and the end of things.

To other peoples, indeed, and to the unaided reason, one of the most difficult of Christian doctrines to understand is that of *creatio ex nihilo:* God's creation of the world not out of Himself, not out of some pre-existent matter or primal chaos, but out of *nothing;* in no other doctrine is the omnipotence of God so plainly stated. The never-dimmed marvelousness of God's creation has its foundation precisely in this fact, that it was called into existence from absolute non-existence.

But what relation, it may be asked, has Nihilism to such a doctrine? It has the relation of denial. "What," says Nietzsche in a statement whose last sentence we have already cited in a different context (p. 31), "does Nihilism mean?—That the highest values are losing their value. There is no goal. There is no answer to the question: 'why?'"* Nihilism, in a word, owes its whole existence to a negation of Christian Truth; it finds the world "absurd," not as a result of dispassionate "research" into the question, but through inability or unwillingness to believe its Christian meaning. Only men who once thought they knew the answer to the question "why?" could be so disillusioned to "discover" that there was no answer after all.

Yet, if Christianity were merely one religion or philosophy among many, its denial would not be a matter of such great import. Joseph de

* *The Will to Power,* p. 8.

Maistre—who was astute in his criticism of the French Revolution, even if his more positive ideas are not to be trusted—saw the point precisely, and at a time when the effects of Nihilism were far less obvious than they are today.

> There have always been some forms of religion in the world and wicked men who opposed them. Impiety was always a crime, too…. *But only in the bosom of the true religion can there be real impiety….* Impiety has never produced in times past the evils which it has brought forth in our day, for its guilt is always directly proportional to the enlightenment which surrounds it…. Although impious men have always existed, there never was before the eighteenth century, and in the heart of Christendom, *an insurrection against God.**

No other religion has affirmed so much and so strongly as Christianity, because its voice is the Voice of God, and its Truth is absolute; and no other religion has had so radical and uncompromising an enemy as Nihilism, for no one can oppose Christianity without doing battle with God Himself.

To fight the very God Who has created him out of nothingness requires, of course, a certain blindness as well as the illusion of strength; but no Nihilist is so blind that he fails to sense, however dimly, the ultimate consequences of his action. The nameless "anxiety" of so many men today testifies to their passive participation in the program of antitheism; the more articulate speak of an "abyss" that seems to have opened up within the heart of man. This "anxiety" and this "abyss" are precisely the nothingness out of which God has called each man into being, and back to which man seems to fall when he denies God, and in consequence, denies his own creation and his own being.

This fear of "falling out of being," as it were, is the most pervasive kind of Nihilism today. It is the constant theme of the arts, and the pre-

* *On God and Society (Essay on the Generative Principle of Political Constitutions and other Human Institutions)*, Henry Regnery Company (Gateway Edition), 1959, pp. 84–86.

vailing note of "absurdist" philosophy. But it is a more conscious Nihilism, the Nihilism of the explicit antitheist, that has been more directly responsible for the calamities of our century. To the man afflicted with such Nihilism, the sense of falling into the abyss, far from ending in passive anxiety and despair, is transformed into a frenzy of Satanic energy that impels him to strike out at the whole of creation and bring it, if he can, plummeting into the abyss with him. Yet in the end a Proudhon, a Bakunin, a Lenin, a Hitler, however great their temporary influence and success, must fail; they must even testify, against their will, to the Truth they would destroy. For their endeavor to *Nihilize* creation, and so annul God's act of creation by returning the world to the very nothingness from which it came, is but an inverted parody of God's creation;* and they, like their father the Devil, are but feeble apes of God who, in their attempt, "prove" the existence of the God they deny, and in their failure testify to His power and glory.

No man, we have said often enough, lives without a god; who then—or what—is the god of the Nihilist? It is *nihil,* nothingness itself—not the nothingness of absence or non-existence, but of apostasy and denial; it is the "corpse" of the "dead God" which so weighs upon the Nihilist. The God hitherto so real and so present to Christian men cannot be disposed of overnight; so absolute a monarch can have no immediate successor. So it is that, at the present moment of man's spiritual history—a moment, admittedly, of crisis and transition—a dead God, a great void, stands at the center of man's faith. The Nihilist wills the world, which once revolved about God, to revolve now about—*nothing*.

Can this be?—an order founded upon nothing? Of course it cannot; it is self-contradiction, it is suicide. But let us not expect coherence from modern thinkers; this is in fact the point modern thought and its Revolution have reached in our time. If it is a point that can be held only for a moment, if it has been reached only to be very quickly

* Cf. Josef Pieper, *The End of Time,* p. 58.

superseded, its reality cannot for all that be denied. There are many signs, which we shall examine in their place, that the world has begun to move out of the "age of Nihilism" since the end of the last great war, and towards some kind of "new age"; but in any case this "new age," if it come, will not see the overcoming of Nihilism, but its perfection. The Revolution reveals its truest face in Nihilism; without repentance—and there has been none—what comes after can only be a mask hiding that same face. Whether overtly in the explicit antitheism of Bolshevism, Fascism, Naziism, or passively in the cult of indifference and despair, "absurdism" and "existentialism," modern man has clearly revealed his resolve to live henceforth without God—that is to say, in a void, in nothingness. Before our century, the well-meaning could still delude themselves that "Liberalism" and "humanism," "science" and "progress," the Revolution itself and the whole path of modern thought were something "positive" and even, in some vague sense, had "God" on their side. It is quite clear now that the Revolution and God can have nothing to do with each other; there is no room in a consistent modern philosophy for God at all. All further modern thought, whatever disguises it may assume, must presuppose this, must be built upon the void left by the "death of God." The Revolution, in fact, cannot be completed until the last vestige of faith in the true God is uprooted from the hearts of men and everyone has learned to live in this void.

From faith comes coherence. The world of faith, which was once the normal world, is a supremely coherent world because in it everything is oriented to God as to its beginning and end, and obtains its meaning in that orientation. Nihilist rebellion, in destroying that world, has inspired a new world: the world of the "absurd." This word, very much in fashion at the present time to describe the plight of contemporary man, has actually, if properly understood, a profound meaning. For if nothingness be the center of the world, then the world, both in its essence and in every detail, is incoherent, it fails to hold together, it is absurd. No one has more clearly and succinctly described this world than Nietzsche, its "prophet," and in the very passage where he first proclaimed its first principle, the "death of God."

> We have killed him (God), you and I! We are all his murderers! But how have we done it? How were we able to drink up the sea? Who gave us the sponge to wipe away the whole horizon? What did we do when we loosened this earth from its sun? Whither does it move now? Wither do we move? Away from all suns? Do we not dash on unceasingly? Backwards, sideways, forwards, in all directions? Is there still an above and below? Do we not stray, as through infinite nothingness? Does not empty space breathe upon us? Has it not become colder? Does not night come on continually, darker and darker?*

Such is the Nihilist universe, in which there is neither up nor down, right nor wrong, true nor false, because there is no longer any point of orientation. Where there was once God, there is now nothing; where there were once authority, order, certainty, faith, there are now anarchy, confusion, arbitrary and unprincipled action, doubt and despair. This is the universe so vividly described by the Swiss Catholic Max Picard, as the world of "the flight from God" and, alternatively, as the world of "discontinuity" and "disjointedness."**

Nothingness, incoherence, antitheism, hatred of truth: what we have been discussing in these pages is more than mere philosophy, more even than a rebellion of man against a God he will no longer serve. A subtle intelligence lies behind these phenomena, and on an intricate plan which philosopher and revolutionary alike merely serve and do not command; we have to do with the work of Satan.

Many Nihilists, indeed, far from disputing this fact, glory in it. Bakunin found himself on the side of "Satan, the eternal rebel, the first freethinker and emancipator of worlds."*** Nietzsche proclaimed

* *The Joyful Wisdom,* #125.
** See Max Picard, *Flight from God,* Henry Regnery Company, 1951; and *Hitler in Our Selves,* Henry Regnery Company, 1947.
*** *God and the State,* p. 2.

himself "Antichrist." Poets, decadents, and the avant-garde in general since the Romantic era have been greatly fascinated by Satanism, and some have tried to make it into a religion. Proudhon in so many words actually invoked Satan:

> Come to me, Lucifer, Satan, whoever you may be! Devil whom the faith of my fathers contrasted with God and the Church. I will act as spokesman for you and will demand nothing of you.*

What is the Orthodox Christian to think of such words? Apologists and scholars of Nihilist thought, when they regard such passages as worthy of comment at all, usually dismiss them as imaginative exaggerations, as bold metaphors to express a perhaps childish "rebellion." To be sure, it must be admitted that there is a juvenile quality in the expression of most of modern "Satanism"; those who so easily invoke Satan and proclaim Antichrist can have very little awareness of the full import of their words, and few intend them to be taken with entire seriousness. This naive bravado reveals, nonetheless, a deeper truth. The Nihilist Revolution stands against authority and order, against Truth, against God; and to do this is, clearly, to stand with Satan. The Nihilist, since he usually believes in neither God nor Satan, may think it mere cleverness to defend, in his fight against God, the age-old enemy of God; but while he may think he is doing no more than playing with words, he is actually speaking the truth.

De Maistre, and later Donoso Cortes, writing in a day when the Church of Rome was more aware of the meaning of the Revolution than it is now, and was still capable of taking a strong stand against it, called the Revolution a Satanic manifestation; and historians smile at them. Fewer, perhaps, smile today when the same phrase is applied—though rarely with full seriousness even now—to National Socialism or Bolshevism; and some may even begin to suspect that there exist forces and causes that have somehow escaped the attention of their enlightened gaze.

* *Idee generale de la revolution;* also *Justice,* III, pp. 433–34 (de Lubac, 173).

IV.

The Nihilist Program

WAR against God, issuing in the proclamation of the reign of nothingness, which means the triumph of incoherence and absurdity, the whole plan presided over by Satan: this, in brief, is the theology and the meaning of Nihilism. But man cannot live by such blatant negation; unlike Satan, he cannot even desire it for its own sake, but only by mistaking it for something positive and good. And in fact no Nihilist—apart from a few moments of frenzy and enthusiasm, or perhaps despair—has ever seen his negation as anything but the means to a higher goal: Nihilism furthers its Satanic ends by means of a positive program. The most violent revolutionaries—a Nechayev or Bakunin, a Lenin or Hitler, and even the demented practitioners of the "propaganda of the deed"—dreamed of the "new order" their violent destructions of the Old Order would make possible; Dada and "anti-literature" seek not the total destruction of art, but the path to a "new" art; the passive Nihilist, in his "existential" apathy and despair, sustains life only by the vague hope that he may yet find some kind of ultimate satisfaction in a world that seems to deny it.

The content of the Nihilist dream is, then, a "positive" one. But truth requires that we view it in proper perspective: not through the rose-colored spectacles of the Nihilist himself, but in the realistic manner our century's intimate acquaintance with Nihilism permits. Armed with the knowledge this acquaintance affords, and with the Christian

Truth which enables us to interpret it aright, we shall attempt to look behind the Nihilist phrases to see the realities they conceal. Seen in this perspective, the very phrases which to the Nihilist seem entirely "positive" appear to the Orthodox Christian in another light, as items in a program quite different from that of Nihilist apologetics.

1. THE DESTRUCTION OF THE OLD ORDER

The first and most obvious item in the program of Nihilism is the destruction of the Old Order. The Old Order was the soil, nourished by Christian Truth, in which men had their roots. Its laws and institutions, and even its customs, were founded in that Truth and dedicated to teaching it; its buildings were erected to the glory of God and were a visible sign of His Order upon earth; even the generally "primitive" (but natural) living conditions served (unintentionally, of course) as a reminder of man's humble place here, of his dependence upon God for even the few earthly blessings he possessed, and of his true home which lies beyond this "vale of tears," in the Kingdom of Heaven. Effective war against God and His Truth requires the destruction of every element of this Old Order; it is here that the peculiarly Nihilist "virtue" of *violence* comes into play.

Violence is no merely incidental aspect of the Nihilist Revolution, but a part of its essence. According to Marxist "dogma," "force is the midwife of every old society pregnant with a new one";* appeals to violence, and even a kind of ecstasy at the prospect of its use, abound in revolutionary literature. Bakunin invoked the "evil passions" and called for the unchaining of "popular anarchy"** in the cause of "universal destruction," and his "Revolutionary Catechism" is the primer of ruthless violence; Marx was fervent in his advocacy of "revolutionary terror" as the one means of hastening the advent of Commu-

---

* Karl Marx, *Capital,* Chicago, Charles Kerr and Company, 1906, Vol. I, p. 824.
** See the citations in E. H. Carr, *op. cit.,* pp. 173, 435; cf. Maximoff, *op. cit.,* pp. 380–81.

nism;* Lenin defined the "dictatorship of the proletariat" (the stage in which the Soviet Union still finds itself) as "a domination that is un-trammeled by law and based on violence."** Demagogic incitement of the masses and the arousing of the basest passions for revolutionary purposes have long been standard Nihilist practice.

The spirit of violence has been most thoroughly incarnated, in our century, by the Nihilist regimes of Bolshevism and National Socialism; it is to these that there have been assigned the principal roles in the Nihilist task of the destruction of the Old Order. The two, whatever their psychological dissimilarities and the historical "accidents" which placed them in opposing camps, have been partners in their frenzied accomplishment of this task. Bolshevism, to be sure, has had the more "positive" role of the two, since it has been able to justify its monstrous crimes by an appeal to a pseudo-Christian, messianic idealism which Hitler scorned; Hitler's role in the Nihilist program was more specialized and provincial, but nonetheless essential.

Even in failure—in fact, *precisely* in the failure of its ostensible aims—Naziism served the cause of this program. Quite apart from the political and ideological benefits which the Nazi interlude in European history gave to the Communist powers (Communism, it is now widely and erroneously believed, if evil in itself, still cannot be as evil as Naziism), Naziism had another, more obvious and direct, function. Goebbels explained this function in his radio broadcasts in the last days of the War.

> The bomb-terror spares the dwellings of neither rich nor poor; before the labor offices of total war the last class barriers have had to go down.... Together with the monuments of culture there crumble also the last obstacles to the fulfillment of our revolutionary

---

* For a synopsis of Marx's views of violence see J. E. LeRossignol, *From Marx to Stalin,* New York, Thomas Y. Crowell Company, 1940, pp. 321–22.
** *Left-Wing Communism,* cited in Stalin, *Foundations of Leninism,* New York, International Publishers, 1932, p. 47. (Or: *The Proletarian Revolution and the Renegade Kautsky,* Little Lenin Library, No. 18, p. 19.)

task. Now that everything is in ruins, we are forced to rebuild Europe. In the past, private possessions tied us to a bourgeois restraint. Now the bombs, instead of killing all Europeans, have only smashed the prison walls which kept them captive…. In trying to destroy Europe's future, the enemy has only succeeded in smashing its past; and with that, everything old and outworn has gone.*

Naziism thus, and its war, have done for Central Europe (and less thoroughly, for Western Europe) what Bolshevism did in its Revolution for Russia: destroyed the Old Order, and thus cleared the way for the building of the "new." Bolshevism then had no difficulty in taking over where Naziism had left off; within a few years the whole of Central Europe had passed under the "dictatorship of the proletariat"—i.e., Bolshevist tyranny—for which Naziism had effectively prepared the way.

The Nihilism of Hitler was too pure, too unbalanced, to have more than a negative, preliminary role to play in the whole Nihilist program. Its role, like the role of the purely negative first phase of Bolshevism, is now finished, and the next stage belongs to a power possessing a more complete view of the whole Revolution, the Soviet power upon which Hitler bestowed, in effect, his inheritance in the words, "the future belongs solely to the stronger Eastern nation."**

2. THE MAKING OF THE "NEW EARTH"

But we do not yet have to do with the ultimate future, with the end of the Revolution; between the Revolution of Destruction and the earthly paradise there lies a stage of transition, known in Marxist doctrine as "the dictatorship of the proletariat." In this stage we may see a second, "constructive" function of violence. The Nihilist Soviet

* Quoted in H. R. Trevor-Roper, *The Last Days of Hitler,* New York, The Macmillan Company, 1947, pp. 50–51.
** Quoted in *Ibid.,* p. 82.

power has been the most ruthless and systematic in developing this stage, but precisely the same work is being accomplished by the Realists of the free world, who have been quite successful in transforming and "simplifying" the Christian tradition into a system for the promotion of worldly "progress." The ideal of Soviet and Western Realists is an identical one, pursued by the former with single-minded fervor, by the latter more spontaneously and sporadically, not always directly by governments but with their encouragement, relying more upon individual initiative and ambition. Realists everywhere envisage a totally "new order," built entirely by men "liberated" from the yoke of God and upon the ruins of an Old Order whose foundation was divine. The Revolution of Nihilism, willed or unwilled, is accepted; and through the labor of workers in all realms, on both sides of the "Iron Curtain," a new, purely human Kingdom is arising, in which its apologists see a "new earth" undreamed of by past ages, an earth totally exploited, controlled, and organized for the sake of man and against the true God.

No place is secure from the encroaching empire of this Nihilism; everywhere men feverishly pursue the work of "progress"—for what reason they do not know, or only very dimly sense. In the free world it is perhaps a *horror vacui* that chiefly impels men into feverish activity that promises forgetfulness of the spiritual emptiness that attends all worldliness; in the Communist world a large role is still played by hatred against real and imagined enemies, but primarily against the God their Revolution has dethroned, a hatred that inspires them to remake the world against Him. In either case it is a cold, inhuman world that men without God are fashioning, a world where there are everywhere organization and efficiency, and nowhere love or reverence. The sterile "purity" and "functionalism" of contemporary architecture are a typical expression of such a world; the same spirit is present in the disease of total planning, for example in "birth control," in experiments that look to the control of heredity and of the mind, in the "welfare state." Some of the apologies for such schemes approach perilously near a strange kind of lucid insanity, wherein precision of detail and technique are united to an appalling insensitivity to the inhuman end these schemes serve.

Nihilist "organization"—the total transformation of the earth and society by machines, modern architecture and design, and the inhuman philosophy of "human engineering" that accompanies them—is a consequence of the unqualified acceptance of the industrialism and technology which we saw in the last chapter as bearers of a worldliness that, if unchecked, must end in tyranny. In it we may see a practical translation of the philosophical development we touched upon in Section I above: the transformation of truth into power. What may seem "harmless" in philosophical pragmatism and skepticism becomes something else again in the "planners" of our own day. For if there is no truth, power knows no limit save that imposed by the medium in which it functions, or by a stronger power opposed to it. The power of contemporary "planners" will find its natural limit, if unopposed, only in a regime of total organization.

Such, indeed, was the dream of Lenin; for before the "dictatorship of the proletariat" comes to an end, "the whole of society will have become one office and one factory, with equal work and equal pay."* In the Nihilist "new earth" all human energy is to be devoted to worldly concerns; the whole human environment and every object in it are to serve the cause of "production" and to remind men that their only happiness lies in this world; there is to be established, in fact, the absolute despotism of worldliness. The artificial world erected by men who will to remove the last vestige of divine influence in the world, and the last trace of faith in men, promises to be so all-encompassing and so omnipresent that it will be all but impossible for men to see, to imagine, or even to hope for anything beyond it. This world, from the Nihilist point of view, will be one of perfect "realism" and total "liberation"; in actual fact it will be the vastest and most efficient prison men have ever known, for—in

* *State and Revolution,* International Publishers, New York, 1935, p. 84.

the precise words of Lenin—"there will be no way of getting away from it, there will be 'nowhere to go'."*

The power of the world, which Nihilists trust as Christians trust their God, can never liberate, it can only enslave; in Christ alone, Who has "overcome the world,"** is there deliverance from that power, even when it shall have become all but absolute.

3. THE FASHIONING OF THE "NEW MAN"

The destruction of the Old Order, however, and the organization of the "new earth" are not the only items in the historical program of Nihilism; they are not, perhaps, even its most important items. They are but the preparation for a work more significant and more ominous than either: the "transformation of man."

This was the dream of the pseudo-Nietzscheans, Hitler and Mussolini, of a "higher humanity" to be forged through a "creative" violence; "this is the mission of our century," said Hitler's propagandist Rosenberg: "out of a new life myth to create a new human type."*** We know from Nazi practice what this "human type" was, and the world would seem to have rejected it as brutal and inhuman. But the "mass change in human nature" to which Marxism looks is an end that is perhaps not very different. Marx and Engels are unequivocal on this subject:

> Both for the production on a mass scale of this communist consciousness, and for the success of the cause itself, the alteration of men on a mass scale is necessary, an alteration which can only take place in a practical movement, a *revolution:* this revolution is necessary, therefore, not only because the ruling class cannot be overthrown in any other way, but also because the class *overthrowing* it

* *Loc. cit.*
** St. John 16:33.
*** *Mythus des 20 Jahrhunderts*, p. 22.

can only in a revolution succeed in ridding itself of all the muck of ages and become fitted to found society anew.*

Putting aside for the moment the question of what kind of men are to be produced by this process, let us note carefully the means utilized: it is again *violence,* which is as necessary to the formation of the "new man" as it is to the building of a "new earth." The two, indeed, are intimately connected in the determinist philosophy of Marx, for "in revolutionary activity, change of self coincides with the change of circumstances."** The change of circumstances, and more to the point, *the process of changing them through revolutionary violence,* transform the revolutionaries themselves. Here Marx and Engels, like their contemporary Nietzsche, and like Lenin and Hitler after them, subscribe to the mystique of violence, seeing a magical change to be wrought in human nature through indulgence of the passions of anger, hatred, resentment, and the will to dominate. In this regard we must make note also of the two World Wars, whose violence has helped to destroy forever the Old Order and the old humanity, rooted in a stable and traditional society, and has had a large role in producing the new uprooted humanity that Marxism idealizes. The thirty years of Nihilist war and revolution between 1914 and 1945 have been an ideal breeding-ground for the "new human type."

It is of course no secret to contemporary philosophers and psychologists that *man himself is changing* in our violent century, under the influence, of course, not only of war and revolution, but also of practically everything else that lays claim to being "modern" and "progressive." We have already cited the most striking forms of Nihilist Vitalism, whose cumulative effect has been to uproot, disintegrate, and "mobilize" the individual, to substitute for his normal stability and rootedness a senseless quest for power and movement, and to replace

* Marx and Engels, *The German Ideology,* Part I, New York, International Publishers, 1947, p. 69.
** *Ibid.,* p. 204 (n. 46).

normal human feeling by a nervous excitability. The work of Nihilist Realism, in practice as in theory, has been parallel and complementary to that of Vitalism: a work of standardization, specialization, simplification, mechanization, dehumanization; its effect has been to "reduce" the individual to the most "primitive" and basic level, to make him in fact the slave of his environment, the perfect workman in Lenin's worldwide "factory."

These observations are commonplace today; a multitude of volumes has been written about them. Many thinkers are able to see the clear connection between the Nihilist philosophy that reduces reality and human nature to the simplest possible terms, and a Nihilist practice that similarly reduces the concrete man; not a few, also, realize the seriousness and the radicalness of this "reduction," even to the extent of seeing in it, as does Erich Kahler, a qualitative change in human nature.

> (The) powerful trend toward the disruption and invalidation of the individual ... manifestly present in the most diverse currents of modern life—economic, technological, political, scientific, educational, psychic and artistic—appears so overwhelming that we are induced to see in it a true mutation, a transformation of human nature.*

But few even of those who realize this much have any real awareness of its profound significance and implications (for these are theological, and so completely outside the scope of any merely empirical analysis), or of a possible remedy (for that must be of the spiritual order). The author just quoted, for example, draws hope from the prospect of a transition into "some supraindividual form of existence," thus revealing that he has no higher wisdom than that of the "spirit of the age," which indeed—as we shall see—has thrown up the ideal of a social "Superman."

---

* Erich Kahler, *The Tower and the Abyss*, New York, George Braziller, Inc., 1957, pp. 225–26.

What, more realistically, is this "mutation," the "new man"? He is the rootless man, discontinuous with a past that Nihilism has destroyed, the raw material of every demagogue's dream; the "free-thinker" and skeptic, closed only to the truth but "open" to each new intellectual fashion because he himself has no intellectual foundation; the "seeker" after some "new revelation," ready to believe anything new because true faith has been annihilated in him; the planner and experimenter, worshipping "fact" because he has abandoned truth, seeing the world as a vast laboratory in which he is free to determine what is "possible"; the autonomous man, pretending to the humility of only asking his "rights," yet full of the pride that expects everything to be given him in a world where nothing is authoritatively forbidden; the man of the moment, without conscience or values and thus at the mercy of the strongest "stimulus"; the "rebel," hating all restraint and authority because he himself is his own and only god; the "mass man," this new barbarian, thoroughly "reduced" and "simplified" and capable of only the most elementary ideas, yet scornful of anyone who presumes to point out the higher things or the real complexity of life.

These men are all one man, the man whose fashioning has been the very purpose of Nihilism. But mere description cannot do justice to this man; one must see his image. And in fact such an image has quite recently been portrayed; it is the image of contemporary painting and sculpture, that which has arisen, for the most part, since the end of the Second World War, as if to give form to the reality produced by the most concentrated era of Nihilism in human history.

The human form, it would seem, has been "rediscovered" in this art; out of the chaos of total abstraction, identifiable shapes emerge. The result, supposedly, is a "new humanism," a "return to man" that is all the more significant in that—unlike so many of the artistic schools of the 20th century—it is not an artificial contrivance whose substance is hidden behind a cloud of irrationalist jargon, but a spontaneous growth that would seem to have deep roots in the soul of contemporary man. In the work, for example, of Alberto Giacometti, Jean

Dubuffet, Francis Bacon, Leon Golub, Jose Luis Cuevas—to take an international sampling*—there seems to be a genuinely "contemporary" art that, without abandoning the disorder and "freedom" of abstraction, turns its attention away from mere escape toward a serious "human commitment."

But what kind of "man" is it to which this art has "returned"? It is certainly not Christian man, man in the image of God, for no "modern" man can believe in him; nor is it the somewhat diluted "man" of the old humanism, whom all "advanced" thinkers regard as discredited and outmoded. It is not even the "man" disfigured and denatured in the earlier "Cubist" and "Expressionist" art of this century; rather, it begins where that art leaves off, and attempts to enter a new realm, to depict a "new man."

To the Orthodox Christian observer, concerned not with what the avant-garde finds fashionable or sophisticated, but with truth, little reflection should be required to penetrate to the secret of this art: there is no question of "man" in it at all; it is an art at once subhuman and demonic. It is not man who is the subject of this art, but some lower creature who has emerged ("arrived" is Giacometti's word for it) from unknown depths.

The bodies this creature assumes (and in all its metamorphoses it is always the same creature) are not necessarily distorted violently; twisted and dismembered as they are, they are often more "realistic" than the figures of man in earlier modern art. This creature, it is clear, is not the victim of some violent attack; rather, *he was born deformed,* he is a genuine "mutation." One cannot but notice the likeness between some of these figures and photographs of the deformed children born recently to thousands of women who had taken the drug Thalidomide during pregnancy; and we have doubtless not seen the last of such monstrous "coincidences."

---

* Numerous examples of this art may be seen in two books by apologists for it: Peter Selz, *New Images of Man,* New York, The Museum of Modern Art, 1959; and Selden Rodman, *The Insiders,* Louisiana State University Press, 1960.

Even more revealing than the bodies of these creatures are the faces. It would be too much to say that these faces express hopelessness; that would be to ascribe to them some trace of humanity which they most emphatically lack. They are the faces, rather, of creatures more or less "adjusted" to the world they know, a world not hostile but entirely alien, not inhuman but "a-human."* The anguish and rage and despair of earlier Expressionists is here frozen, as it were, and cut off from a world to which they had at least the relation of denial, so as to make a world of their own. Man, in this art, is no longer even a caricature of himself; he is no longer portrayed in the throes of spiritual death, ravaged by the hideous Nihilism of our century that attacks, not just the body and soul, but the very idea and nature of man. No, all this has passed; the crisis is over; man is dead. The new art celebrates the birth of a new species, the creature of the lower depths, subhumanity.

We have dealt with this art at a length perhaps disproportionate to its intrinsic value, because it offers concrete and unmistakable evidence—for him who has eyes to see—of a reality which, expressed abstractly, seems frankly incredible. It is easy to dismiss as fantasy the "new humanity" foreseen by a Hitler or a Lenin; and even the plans of those quite respectable Nihilists among us today who calmly discuss the scientific breeding of a "biological superman," or project a utopia for "new men" to be developed by the narrowest "modern education" and a strict control of the mind, seem remote and only faintly ominous.

But confronted with the actual image of a "new man," an image brutal and loathsome beyond imagination, and at the same time so unpremeditated, consistent, and widespread in contemporary art, one is caught up short, and the full horror of the contemporary state of man strikes one a blow one is not likely soon to forget.

* The term is Erich Kahler's, in *op. cit.,* p. 15.

V.

Beyond Nihilism

T HE image of the "new man" presented in these pages has been exclusively a negative one. Many students of the contemporary state of man, while perhaps admitting the truth of some of our observations, would condemn them as a whole for being "one-sided." In all justice, then, we must examine the other side, the "positive" view.

And indeed it cannot be questioned that beside the current of despair, disillusionment, and "a-humanity" that we have described as emerging from the era of Nihilism, there has been developing a parallel current of optimism and idealism that has produced its own "new men." These are the young men both idealistic and practical, ready and anxious to cope with the difficult problems of the day, to spread the American or the Soviet ideal (or the more universal ideal that stands above both) to "backward" countries; enthusiastic scientists, pushing back "frontiers" everywhere in the undeniably "exciting" research and experimentation being conducted today; pacifists and non-violent idealists, crusading in the cause of peace, brotherhood, world-unity, and the overcoming of age-old hatreds; young writers, "angry" for the cause of justice and equality and preaching—as best they can in this sorry world—a new message of joy and creativity; even the artists whose image of man we have mercilessly attacked, for it is surely their intention to condemn the world that produced this man and so point the way beyond him; and the great numbers of more ordinary young people who are enthusiastic to be alive in this "exciting" time, sincere, well-meaning, looking with confidence and optimism to the future, to a world that may at least know happiness instead of misery. The older generation, itself too scarred from the era of Nihilism it has passed through to share fully the enthusiasm of the young, has high hopes for them; is it not just possible that, if the "spirit of the age" is favorable, their dreams may after all be realized?

Without as yet answering this question we must ask another, more fundamental, question: of what nature are the faith and hope that inspire these dreams? The answer is evident: they are entirely a worldly faith and hope. Artistic and scientific novelties, prosperity and comfort, new worlds for exploration, "peace," "brotherhood," and "joy" as the popular mind understands them: these are the goods of the world that pass away, and if they are pursued with the single-minded devotion which the optimistic "new man" of today devotes to them, they are spiritually harmful. Man's true and eternal home is not in this world; the true peace and love and joy of Christ, which the believer knows even in this life, are of an entirely different dimension from the worldly parodies of them which fill the "new man" with vain hopes.

The existence of this "new man," whose faith and hope are directed solely to this world, is but another proof of the success of the Nihilist program. The "new man" in his "positive" form is taken from the same photograph of which the subhumanity we have described is the negative. In the negative he is seen as defeated and denatured by an inhuman world; the pessimism and despair of this image—and this is their only positive significance—are a last feeble protest against the work of Nihilism, at the same time that they are a testimony to its success. In the positive, the "new man" has set about to change the world, and at the same time to change his own attitude to one of acceptance of the modern world which, though imperfect, is the only one he knows; in this image there is no more conflict, for man is well on the way to being thoroughly refashioned and reoriented, and thus perfectly "adjusted" to the new world. The two images are one in issuing from the death of man as he has hitherto been known—man living on earth as a pilgrim, looking to Heaven as his true home—and in pointing to the birth of a "new man" solely of the earth, knowing neither hope nor despair save over the things of this world.

Between them, the positive and negative images of the "new man" sum up the state of contemporary man, the man in whom worldliness has triumphed over faith. At the same time, they are a sign of transition, a presage of a major change in the "spirit of the age." In the negative image the apostasy from Christian Truth which primarily characterizes the modern age seems to have reached its limit; God being "dead," the man created in His image has lost his nature and fallen into subhumanity. In the positive image, on the other hand, a new movement seems to have begun; man has discovered his new nature, that of a creature of the earth. The age of denial and Nihilism, having gone as far as it could, is over; the "new man" no longer has enough interest in Christian Truth to deny it; his whole attention is directed to this world.

The new age, which many call a "post-Christian" age, is at the same time the age "beyond Nihilism"—a phrase that expresses at once a fact and a hope. The fact this phrase expresses is that Nihilism, being negative in essence even if positive in aspiration, owing its whole energy to its passion to destroy Christian Truth, comes to the end of its program in the production of a mechanized "new earth" and a dehumanized "new man": Christian influence over man and over society having been effectively obliterated, Nihilism must retire and give way to another, more "constructive" movement capable of acting from autonomous and positive motives. This movement, which we shall describe in the next chapter under the name of Anarchism, takes up the Revolution at the point where Nihilism leaves off and attempts to bring the movement which Nihilism began to its logical conclusion.

The hope contained in the phrase, "beyond Nihilism," is the naive one that it has a spiritual as well as an historical reference, that the new age is to see the overcoming of Nihilism and not merely its obsolescence. The god of Nihilism, nothingness, is an emptiness, a vacuum waiting to be filled; those who have lived in this vacuum and acknowledged nothingness as their god cannot but seek a new god and hope that he will lead them out of the age and the power of Nihilism. It is such people who, anxious to draw some positive significance from their situation, and unwilling to believe that the Nihilism through which our age has passed can be entirely unfruitful, have constructed an apology in which Nihilism, however evil or unfortunate it may be in itself, is seen as the necessary means to an end beyond itself, as destruction preceding reconstruction, as darkness preceding the dawn. If the present darkness, uncertainty, and suffering are unpleasant—so this apology continues—they are at the same time beneficial and purifying; stripped bare of illusions, in the midst of a "dark night" of doubt and despair, one can only suffer these trials in patience and remain "open" and "receptive" to what the omnipotential future may bring. Nihilism, it is presumed, is the apocalyptic sign of the advent of a new and better age.

This apology is nearly universal, and is capable of being adapted to innumerable contemporary viewpoints. Goebbels' view of the ultimately "positive" meaning of National Socialism, which we cited in the preceding section, is perhaps the most extreme of such adaptations. Other more "spiritual" versions of it have been common since the great crisis in thought provoked by the French Revolution. Poets, would-be "prophets," and occultists, as well as the more prosaic men whom these visionaries have influenced, while agonizing over the disorders of their times, have found comfort in the thought that they have been a blessing in disguise. W. B. Yeats may again be cited as typical in this attitude.

> Dear predatory birds, prepare for war.... Love war because of its horror, that belief may be changed, civilization renewed.... Belief comes from shock.... Belief is renewed continually in the ordeal of death.*

More specifically, much the same attitude underlies contemporary hopes with regard to the Soviet Union. Being "realistic," most men accept the social, political, and economic transformations wrought by

---

* *A Vision,* 1937, pp. 52–53.

Marxism, while deprecating its violent means and its extremist ideology; at the same time, being optimistic and open to a better turn of affairs, men have welcomed the "thaw" that set in with the death of Stalin, hoping to see in it the first signs of a far-reaching transformation of the Marxist ideal. From "coexistence," perhaps, one may proceed to cooperation, and finally to harmony.

Such ideas are the result of a basic misconception of the nature of the modern Revolution; Nihilism is but one side of this Revolution. Violence and negation are, to be sure, a preliminary work; but this work is only part of a much larger plan whose end promises to be, not something better, but something incomparably worse than the age of Nihilism. If in our own times there are signs that the era of violence and negation is passing, this is by no means because Nihilism is being "overcome" or "outgrown," but because its work is all but completed and its usefulness is at an end. The Revolution, perhaps, begins to move out of its malevolent phase and into a more "benevolent" one—not because it has changed its will or its direction, but because it is nearing the attainment of the ultimate goal which it has never ceased to pursue; fat with its success, it can prepare to relax in the enjoyment of this goal.

The last hope of modern man is in fact but another of his illusions; the hope for a new age "beyond Nihilism" is itself an expression of the last item in the program of the Revolution. It is by no means Marxism alone that promotes this program. There is no major power today whose government is not "revolutionary," no one in a position of authority or influence whose criticism of Marxism goes beyond the proposal of better means to an end that is equally "revolutionary"; to disown the ideology of the Revolution in the contemporary "intellectual climate" would be, quite clearly, to condemn oneself to political powerlessness. There is no clearer proof than this of the anti-Christian spirit of our age—the profoundest anti-Christianity being, of course, the pseudo-Christianity which is the goal of the Revolution.

Nihilism itself, in coming to the end of its own program, points to this goal that lies beyond it; that is the real meaning of the Nihilist apology of Yeats and others. But again, it is perhaps in Nietzsche, that uncanny "prophet" who knew everything about Nihilism except its ultimate meaning, that this idea receives its most striking expression.

> Under certain circumstances, the appearance of the *extremest* form of Pessimism and actual *Nihilism* might be the sign of a process of incisive and most essential growth, and of mankind's transit into completely new conditions of existence. *This is what I have understood.**

Beyond Nihilism there is to be a "transvaluation of all values":

> With this formula a *counter-movement* finds expression, in regard to both a principle and a mission; a movement which in some remote future will supersede this perfect Nihilism; but which nevertheless regards it as a *necessary step,* both logically and psychologically, towards its own advent, and which positively cannot come, except *on top of* and *out of it.* **

Strangely enough, the very same idea is expressed in the totally different context of Lenin's thought, where, after the exaltation of the Nihilist idea of the universal "factory," he continues:

> But this "factory" discipline, which the proletariat will extend to the whole of society after the defeat of the capitalists and the overthrow of the exploiters, is by no means our ideal, or our final aim. It is but a *foothold* necessary for the radical cleansing of society of all the hideousness and foulness of capitalist exploitation, *in order to advance further.****

It is this "further" point, which Nietzsche and Lenin are at one in describing as "completely new conditions of existence," that is the ultimate goal of the Revolution. This goal, since it is in a certain sense "beyond Nihilism," and also because it is a large topic in itself, re-

---

* *The Will to Power,* p. 92.
** *Ibid.,* p. 2.
*** *State and Revolution,* p. 84.

quires a separate chapter. To conclude this chapter and our discussion of Nihilism proper, it will be sufficient merely to suggest its nature, and thus establish the general framework of our exposition in the next chapter; this goal may be viewed as a three-fold corollary of Nihilist thought.

First, the corollary of the Nihilist annihilation of the Old Order is the conception of a "new age"—"new" in an absolute, and not a relative, sense. The age about to begin is not to be merely the latest, or even the greatest, of a series of ages, but the inauguration of a whole new time; it is set up against all that has hitherto been. "It may be," said Nietzsche in a letter of 1884, "that I am *the first* to light upon an idea which will divide the history of mankind in two";* as the consequence of this idea, "all who are born after us belong to a higher history than any history hitherto."** Nietzsche is, of course, blinded by his pride; he made no original "discovery" but only found words for what had been "in the air" already for some time. Precisely the same idea, in fact, was expressed twelve years earlier by Dostoyevsky in the person of Kirillov, the most extreme of the "possessed":

> Everything will be new … then they will divide history into two parts: from the gorilla to the annihilation of God, and from the annihilation of God to the transformation of the earth, and of man physically.***

Here there is already suggested the second corollary of Nihilist thought. The Nihilist rebellion and antitheism responsible for the "death of God" give rise to the idea that is to inaugurate the "new age": the transformation of man himself into a god. "Dead are all the gods," says Nietzsche's Zarathustra: "now do we desire the superman to live."**** The "murder" of God is a deed too great to leave men un-

* Quoted in Henri de Lubac, *The Drama of Atheist Humanism,* p. 24.
** *The Joyful Wisdom,* #125.
*** *The Possessed,* Part I, Ch. 3.
**** *Thus Spake Zarathustra.*

changed: "Shall we not ourselves have to become gods, merely to seem worthy of it?"* In Kirillov, the Superman is the "Mangod," for in his logic, "if there is no God, then I am God."**

It is this idea of the "Superman" that underlies and inspires the conception of the "transformation of man," alike in the Realism of Marx and in the Vitalism of numerous occultists and artists. The various conceptions of the "new man" are, as it were, a series of preliminary sketches of the Superman. For just as nothingness, the god of Nihilism, is but an emptiness and expectancy looking to fulfillment in the revelation of some "new god," so too the "new man," whom Nihilism has deshaped, reduced, and left without character, without faith, without orientation—this "new man," whether viewed as "positive" or "negative," has become "mobile" and "flexible," "open" and "receptive," he is passive material awaiting some new discovery or revelation or command that is to remold him finally into his definitive shape.

Finally, the corollary of the Nihilist annihilation of authority and order is the conception—adumbrated in all the myths of a "new order"—of an entirely new species of order, an order which its most ardent defenders do not hesitate to call "Anarchy." The Nihilist State, in the Marxist myth, is to "wither away," leaving a world-order that is to be unique in human history, and which it would be no exaggeration to call the "millennium."

A "new age" ruled by "Anarchy" and populated by "Supermen": this is the Revolutionary dream that has stirred men into performing the incredible drama of modern history. It is an "apocalyptic" dream, and they are quite correct who see in it a strange inversion of the Christian hope in the Kingdom of Heaven. But that is no excuse for the "sympathy" so often accorded at least the more "sincere" and "noble" Revolutionaries and Nihilists; this is one of the pitfalls we found it necessary to warn against at the very beginning of this chapter. In a world

* *The Joyful Wisdom,* #125.
** *The Possessed,* Part III, Ch. 6.

thinly balanced on the edge of chaos, where all truth and nobility seem to have vanished, the temptation is great among the well-meaning but naive to seek out certain of the undoubtedly striking figures who have populated the modern intellectual landscape, and—in ignorance of genuine standards of truth and spirituality—to magnify them into spiritual "giants" who have spoken a word which, though "unorthodox," is at least "challenging." But the realities of this world and of the next are too rigorous to permit such vagueness and liberalism. Good intentions too easily go astray, genius and nobility are too often perverted; and the corruption of the best produces, not the second best, but the worst. One must grant genius and fervor, and even a certain nobility to a Marx, a Proudhon, a Nietzsche; but theirs is the nobility of Lucifer, the first among the angels who, wishing to be even more than he was, fell from that exalted position into the abyss. Their vision, in which some would see a profounder kind of Christianity, is the vision of the Reign of Antichrist, the Satanic imitation and inversion of the Kingdom of God. All Nihilists, but preeminently those of the greatest genius and the broadest vision, are the prophets of Satan; refusing to use their talents in the humble service of God, *They have waged war against God with His own gifts.**

It can hardly be denied, and a sober look at the transformations the world and man have undergone in the last two centuries can only confirm the fact, that the war of the enemies of God has been successful; its ultimate victory, in fact, seems imminent. But what can "victory" mean in such a war? What kind of "peace" can a humanity know that has been learning so long the lessons of violence? In the Christian life, we know, there is a harmony of means and ends. Through prayer and a devout life, and through the Sacraments of the Church, the Christian is changed, by the Grace of God, to become more like his Lord and thus more worthy to participate in the Kingdom He has prepared for those who truly follow Him. Those who are His are known by the fruits they

---

* De Maistre, *op. cit.,* p. 85, quoting a phrase of (Saint) Louis IX.

bear: patience, humility, meekness, obedience, peace, joy, love, kindness, forgiveness—fruits which at one and the same time prepare for and already share in the fullness of that Kingdom. End and means are one; what is begun in this life is perfected in the life to come.

In the same way there is a "harmony" in the works of Satan; the "virtues" of his servants are consistent with the ends they serve. Hatred, pride, rebelliousness, discord, violence, unscrupulous use of power: these will not magically disappear when the Revolutionary Kingdom is finally realized on earth; they will rather be intensified and perfected. If the Revolutionary goal "beyond Nihilism" is described in precisely contrary terms, and if Nihilists actually see it as a reign of "love," "peace," and "brotherhood," that is because Satan is the ape of God and even in denial must acknowledge the source of that denial, and—more to the present point—because men have been so changed by the practice of the Nihilist "virtues," and by acceptance of the Nihilist transformation of the world, that they actually begin to live in the Revolutionary Kingdom and to see everything as Satan sees it, as the contrary of what it is in the eyes of God.

What lies "beyond Nihilism" and has been the profoundest dream of its greatest "prophets," is by no means the overcoming of Nihilism, but its culmination. The "new age," being largely the work of Nihilism, will be, in substance, nothing different from the Nihilist era we know. To believe otherwise, to look for salvation to some new "development," whether brought about by the inevitable forces of "progress" or "evolution" or some romantic "dialectic," or supplied gratuitously from the treasury of the mysterious "future" before which modern men stand in superstitious awe—to believe this is to be the victim of a monstrous delusion. Nihilism is, most profoundly, a spiritual disorder, and it can be overcome only by spiritual means; and there has been no attempt whatever in the contemporary world to apply such means.

The Nihilist disease is apparently to be left to "develop" to its very end; the goal of the Revolution, originally the hallucination of a few fevered minds, has now become the goal of humanity itself. Men have become weary; the Kingdom of God is too distant, the Orthodox Christian way is too narrow and arduous. The Revolution has captured the "spirit of the age," and to go against this powerful current is more than modern men can do, for it requires precisely the two things most thoroughly annihilated by Nihilism: Truth and faith.

To end our discussion of Nihilism on such a note as this is, surely, to lay ourselves open to the charge that we possess a Nihilism of our own; our analysis, it may be argued, is "pessimistic" in the extreme. Categorically rejecting almost everything held valuable and true by modern man, we seem to be as thorough in denial as the most extreme of Nihilists.

And indeed the Christian is, in a certain sense—in an ultimate sense—a "Nihilist"; for to him, in the end, the world is nothing, and God is all. This is, of course, the precise opposite of the Nihilism we have examined here, where God is nothing and the world is all; that is a Nihilism that proceeds from the Abyss, and the Christian's is a "Nihilism" that proceeds from abundance. The true Nihilist places his faith in things that pass away and end in nothing; all "optimism" on this foundation is clearly futile. The Christian, renouncing such vanity places his faith in the one thing that will not pass away, the Kingdom of God.

To him who lives in Christ, of course, many of the goods of this world may be given back, and he may enjoy them even while realizing their evanescence; but they are not needful, they are truly nothing to him. He who does not live in Christ, on the other hand, already lives in the Abyss, and not all the treasures of this world can ever fill his emptiness.

But it is a mere literary device to call the nothingness and poverty of the Christian "Nihilism"; they are rather fullness, abundance, joy beyond imagining. And it is only one full of such abundance who can squarely face the Abyss to which Nihilism has conducted men. The most extreme denier, the most disillusioned of men, can only exist if he exempt at least one illusion from his destructive analysis. This fact is indeed the psychological root of that "new age" in which the most thorough Nihilist must place all his hope; he who cannot believe in Christ must, and will, believe in Antichrist.

But if Nihilism has its historical end in the Reign of Antichrist, it has its ultimate and spiritual end beyond even that final Satanic manifestation; and in this end, which is Hell, Nihilism meets its final defeat. The Nihilist is defeated, not merely because his dream of paradise ends in eternal misery; for the thorough Nihilist—unlike his opposite, the Anarchist—is too disillusioned really to believe in that paradise, and too full of rage and rebellion to do anything but destroy it in its turn, if it ever came into existence. The Nihilist is defeated, rather, because in Hell his deepest wish, *the Nihilization of God, of creation, and of himself,* is proved futile. Dostoyevsky well described, in the words of the dying Father Zossima, this ultimate refutation of Nihilism.

> There are some who remain proud and fierce even in hell, in spite of their certain knowledge and contemplation of the absolute truth; there are some fearful ones who have given themselves over to Satan and his proud spirit entirely. For such, hell is voluntary and ever consuming; they are tortured by their own choice. For they have cursed themselves, cursing God and life…. They cannot behold the living God without hatred, and they cry out that the God of life should be annihilated, that God should destroy Himself and His own creation. And they will burn in the fire of their own wrath for ever and yearn for death and annihilation. But they will not attain to death.*

It is the great and invincible truth of Christianity that *there is no annihilation;* all Nihilism is in vain. God may be fought: that is one of the meanings of the modern age; but He may not be conquered, and He may not be escaped: His Kingdom shall endure eternally, and all who reject the call to His Kingdom must burn in the flames of Hell forever.

* *The Brothers Karamazov,* Book VI, Ch. 3.

It has, of course, been a primary intention of Nihilism to abolish Hell and the fear of Hell from men's minds, and no one can doubt their success; Hell has become, for most people today, a folly and a superstition, if not a "sadistic" fantasy. Even those who still believe in the Liberal "heaven" have no room in their universe for any kind of Hell.

Yet, strangely, modern men have an understanding of Hell that they do have not of Heaven; the word and the concept have a prominent place in contemporary art and thought. No sensitive observer is unaware that men, in the Nihilist era more than ever before, have made of earth an image of Hell; and those who are aware of dwelling in the Abyss do not hesitate to call their state Hell. The torture and miseries of this life are indeed a foretaste of Hell, even as the joys of a Christian life—joys which the Nihilist cannot even imagine, so remote are they from his experience—are a foretaste of Heaven.

But if the Nihilist has a dim awareness, even here, of the meaning of Hell, he has no idea of its full extent, which cannot be experienced in this life; even the most extreme Nihilist, while serving the demons and even invoking them, has not had the spiritual sight necessary to see them as they are. The Satanic spirit, the spirit of Hell, is always disguised in this world; its snares are set along a broad path that may seem pleasant, or at least exciting, to many; and Satan offers, to those who follow his path, the consoling thought and hope of ultimate extinction. If, despite the consolations of Satan, no follower of his is very "happy" in this life, and if in the last days (of which the calamities of our century are a small preview) there "shall be great tribulation, such as was not since the beginning of the world to this time"—still it is only in the next life that the servants of Satan will realize the full bitterness of hopeless misery.

The Christian believes in Hell and fears its fire—not earthly fire, as clever unbelief would have it, but fire infinitely more painful because, like the bodies with which men shall rise on the Last Day, it shall be spiritual and unending. The world reproaches the Christian for believing in such an unpleasant reality; but it is neither perversity nor "sadism" that leads him to do so, but rather faith and experience. Only he, perhaps, can fully believe in Hell who fully believes in Heaven and life in God; for only he who has some idea of that life can have any notion of what its absence will mean.

For most men today "life" is a small thing, a fleeting thing of small affirmation and small denial, veiled in comforting illusions and the hopeful prospect of ultimate nothingness; such men will know nothing of Hell until they live in it. But God loves even such men too much to allow them simply to "forget" Him and "pass away" into nothingness, out of His Presence which alone is life to men; He offers, even to those in Hell, His Love which is torment to those who have not prepared themselves in this life to receive it. Many, we know, are tested and purified in those flames and made fit by them to dwell in the Kingdom of Heaven; but others, with the demons for whom Hell was made, must dwell there eternally.

There is no need, even today when men seem to have become too weak to face the truth, to soften the realities of the next life; to those—be they Nihilists or more moderate humanists—who presume to fathom the Will of the Living God, and to judge Him for His "cruelty," one may answer with an unequivocal assertion of something in which most of them profess to believe: the dignity of man. God has called us, not to the modern "heaven" of repose and sleep, but to the full and deifying glory of the sons of God; and if we, whom our God thinks worthy to receive it, reject this call,—then better for us the flames of Hell, the torment of that last and awful proof of man's high calling and of God's unquenchable Love for all men, than the nothingness to which men of small faith, and the Nihilism of our age, aspire. Nothing less than Hell is worthy of man, if he be not worthy of Heaven.

EUGENE ROSE'S PROPOSED OUTLINE OF
THE KINGDOM OF MAN AND THE KINGDOM OF GOD

Introduction: The Contemporary Situation of the World and the Church

Part I: *The Two Kingdoms, Their Source and Their Power*
    Chapter One: The two loves, and the two faiths: the world, and God.
    Chapter Two: The power of the world, and the power of Christ.

Part II: *The Kingdom of Man in the Modern Age*
    Chapter Three: An Orthodox Christian interpretation of the modern age.
    Chapter Four: The worldly idols of the modern age.
        I. Culture/Civilization, judged by Orthodox Christian spirituality.
        II. Science/Rationalism, judged by Divine Wisdom.
        III. History/Progress, judged by the Orthodox Christian theology of history.

Part III: *The Old Order and the "New Order"*
    Chapter Five: The Old Order: The Orthodox Christian Empire.
    Chapter Six: The advent of the "New Order": the Revolution of the modern age.
    Chapter Seven: The root of the Revolution: Nihilism.
    Chapter Eight: The goal of the Revolution: the Anarchist Millennium.

Part IV: *Orthodox Christian Spirituality and the "New Spirituality"*
    (About four chapters.)

Part V: *The End of the Two Kingdoms*
    Chapter Thirteen: The "New Christianity" and the Reign of Antichrist.
    Chapter Fourteen: The Kingdom of Heaven.

Appendix

The Philosophy of the Absurd

EDITOR'S NOTE: While working on The Kingdom of Man and the Kingdom of God, *Eugene Rose wrote the following as a separate essay. We present this essay here not only because it was written at about the same time as his chapter on Nihilism, but also because its theme ties in so closely with that of the present book. It offers profound insights into the absurdist philosophy that continues to grip the minds of many—minds already shaped by the nihilistic undercurrent of our times.*

THE present age is, in a profound sense, an age of absurdity. Poets and dramatists, painters and sculptors proclaim and depict the world as a disjointed chaos, and man as a dehumanized fragment of that chaos. Politics, whether of the right, the left, or the center, can no longer be viewed as anything but an expedient whereby universal disorder is given, for the moment, a faint semblance of order; pacifists and militant crusaders are united in an absurd faith in the feeble powers of man to remedy an intolerable situation by means which can only make it worse. Philosophers and other supposedly responsible men in governmental, academic, and ecclesiastical circles, when they do not retreat behind the impersonal and irresponsible façade of specialization or bureaucracy, usually do no more than rationalize the incoherent state of contemporary man and his world, and counsel a futile "commitment" to a discredited humanist optimism, to a hopeless stoicism, to blind experimentation and irrationalism, or to "commitment" itself, a suicidal faith in "faith."

But art, politics, and philosophy today are only reflections of life, and if they have become absurd it is because, in large measure, life has become so. The most striking example of absurdity in life in recent times was, of course, Hitler's "new order," wherein a supposedly normal, civilized man could be at one and the same time an accomplished and moving interpreter of Bach (as was Himmler) and a skilled murderer of millions, or who might arrange a tour of an extermination camp to coincide with a concert series or an exhibition of art. Hitler himself, indeed, was the absurd man *par excellence*, passing from nothingness to world rule and back to nothingness in the space of a dozen years, leaving as his monument nothing but a shattered world, owing his meaningless success to the fact that he, the emptiest of men, personified the emptiness of the men of his time.

Hitler's surrealist world is now a thing of the past; but the world has by no means passed out of the age of absurdity, but rather into a more advanced—though temporarily quieter—stage of the same disease. Men have invented a weapon to express, better that Hitler's gospel of destruction, their own incoherence and nihilism; and in its shadow men stand paralyzed, between the extremes of an external power and an internal powerlessness equally without precedent. At the same time, the poor and "underprivileged" of the world have awakened to conscious life, and seek abundance and privilege; those who already possess them waste their lives in the pursuit of vain things, or become disillusioned and die of boredom and despair, or commit senseless crimes. The whole world, it almost seems, is divided into those who lead meaningless, futile lives without being aware of it, and those who, being aware of it, are driven to madness and suicide.

It is unnecessary to multiply examples of a phenomenon of which everyone is aware. Suffice it to say that these examples are typical, and even the most extreme of them are but advanced forms of the disorder which surrounds every one of us today and which, if we know not how to combat it, takes up residence in our hearts. Ours is an age of absurdity, in which the totally irreconcilable exists side by side, even in the same soul; where nothing seems to any purpose; where things fall apart because they have no center to hold them together. It is true, of course, that the business of daily life seems to proceed as usual—though at a suspiciously feverish pace—men manage to "get along," to live from day to day. But that is because they do not, or will not think; and one can hardly blame them for that, for the realities of the present day are not pleasant ones. Still, it is only the person who does think, who does ask what, beneath the distractions of daily life, is really happening in the world—it is only such a person who can feel even remotely "at home" in the strange world we live in today, or can feel that this age is, after all, "normal."

It is *not* a "normal" age in which we live; whatever their exaggerations and errors, however false their explanations, however contrived their world-view, the "advanced" poets, artists, and thinkers of the age are at least right in one respect: there is something frightfully wrong with the contemporary world. This is the first lesson we may learn from absurdism.

For absurdism is a profound symptom of the spiritual state of contemporary man, and if we know how to read it correctly we may learn much of that state. But this brings us to the most important of the initial difficulties to be disposed of before we can speak of the absurd. Can it be understood at all? The absurd is, by its very nature, a subject that lends itself to careless or sophistical treatment; and such treatment has indeed been given it, not only by the artists who are carried away by it, but by the supposedly serious thinkers and critics who attempt to explain or justify it. In most of the works on contemporary "existentialism," and in the apologies for modern art and drama, it would seem that intelligence has been totally abandoned, and critical standards are replaced by a vague "sympathy" or "involvement," and by extra-logical if not illogical arguments that cite the "spirit of the age" or some vague "creative" impulse or an indeterminate "awareness"; but these are not arguments, they are at best rationalizations, at worst mere jargon. If we follow that path we may end with a greater "appreciation" of absurdist art, but hardly with any profounder understanding of it. Absurdism, indeed, may not be understood at all in its own terms; for understanding is coherence, and that is the very opposite of absurdity. If we are to understand the absurd at all, it must be from a standpoint outside absurdity, a standpoint from which a word like "understanding" has a meaning; only thus may we cut through the intellectual fog within which absurdism conceals itself, discouraging coherent and rational attack by its own assault on reason and coherence. We must, in short, take a stand within a faith opposed to the absurdist faith and attack it in the name of a truth of which it denies the existence. In the end we shall find that absurdism, quite against its will, offers its own testimony to this faith and this truth which are—let us state at the outset—Christian.

The philosophy of the absurd is, indeed, nothing original in itself; it is entirely negation, and its character is determined, absolutely and entirely, by that which it attempts to negate. The absurd could not even be conceived except in relation to something considered *not* to be absurd; the fact that the world fails to make sense could occur only to men who have once believed, and have good reason to believe, that it does make sense. Absurdism cannot be understood apart from its Christian origins.

Christianity is, supremely, coherence, for the Christian God has ordered everything in the universe, both with regard to everything else and with regard to Himself, Who is the beginning and end of all creation; and the Christian whose faith is genuine finds this divine coherence in every aspect of his life and thought. For the absurdist, everything falls apart, including his own philosophy, which can only be a short-lived phenomenon; for the Christian, everything holds together and is coherent, including those things which in themselves are incoherent. The incoherence of the absurd is, in the end, part of a larger coherence; if it were not, there would be little point in speaking of it at all.

The second of the initial difficulties in approaching the absurd concerns the precise manner of approach. It will not do—if we wish to understand it—to dismiss absurdism as mere error and self-contradiction; it is these, to be sure, but it is also much more. No competent thinker, surely, can be tempted to take seriously any absurdist claim to truth; no matter from which side one approaches it, absurdist philosophy is nothing but self-contradiction. To proclaim ultimate meaninglessness, one must believe that this phrase has a meaning, and thus one denies it in affirming it; to assert that "there is no truth," one must believe in the truth of this statement, and so again affirm what one denies. Absurdist philosophy, it is clear, is not to be taken seriously as philosophy; all its objective statements must be reinterpreted imaginatively, and often subjectively. Absurdism, in fact—as we shall see—is not a product of the intellect at all, but of the will.

The philosophy of the absurd, while implicit in a large number of contemporary works of art, is fortunately quite explicit—if we know how to interpret it—in the writings of Nietzsche; for his nihilism is precisely the root from which the tree of absurdity has grown. In Nietzsche we may read the philosophy of the absurd; in his older contemporary Dostoevsky we may see described the sinister implications which Nietzsche, blind to the Christian truth which is the only remedy for the absurd view of life, failed to see. In these two writers, living at the dividing point between two worlds, when the world of coherence based on Christian truth was being shattered and the world of the absurd based on its denial was coming into being, we may find almost everything there is of importance to know about the absurd.

The absurdist revelation, after a long period of underground germination, bursts into the open in the two striking phrases of Nietzsche so often quoted: "God is dead" means simply, that faith in God is dead in the hearts of modern men; and "there is no truth" means that men have abandoned the truth revealed by God upon which all European thought and institutions once were based. They have abandoned it because they no longer find it credible. Both statements are indeed true of what has, since Nietzsche's time, become the vast majority of those who were once Christian. It is true of the atheists and satanists who profess to be content or ecstatic at their own lack of faith and rejection of truth; it is equally true of the less pretentious multitudes in whom the sense of spiritual reality has simply evaporated, whether this event be expressed in indifference to spiritual reality, in that spiritual confusion and unrest so widespread today, or in any of the many forms of pseudo-religion that are but masks for indifference and confusion. And even over that ever-decreasing minority who still believe, inwardly as well as outwardly, for whom the other world is more real than this world—even over these the shadow of the "death of God" has fallen and made the world a different and a strange place.

Nietzsche, in the *Will to Power,* comments very succinctly on the meaning of nihilism:

> What does nihilism mean?—That the highest values are losing their value. There is no goal. There is no answer to the question: "Why?"

Everything, in short, has become questionable. The magnificent certainty we see in the Fathers and Saints of the Church, and in all true believers, that refers everything, whether in thought or life, back to God, seeing everything as beginning and ending in Him, everything as His will—this certainty and faith that once held society and the world and man himself together, are now gone, and the questions for which men once had learned to find the answers in God, now have—for most men—no answers.

There have been, of course, other forms of coherence than Christianity, and forms of incoherence other than modern nihilism and absurdity. In them human life makes sense, or fails to make sense, but only to a limited degree. Men who believe and follow, for example, the traditional Hindu or Chinese view of things, possess a measure of truth and of the peace that comes from truth—but not absolute truth, and not the "peace that passes all understanding" that proceeds only from absolute truth; and those who fall away from this relative truth and peace have lost something real, but they have not lost everything, as has the apostate Christian. Never has such disorder reigned in the heart of man and in the world today; but this is precisely because man has fallen away from a truth and a coherence that have been revealed in their fullness only in Christ. Only the Christian God is at the same time all power and all love; only the Christian God, through His love has promised men immortality and, through His power to fulfill that promise, has prepared a Kingdom in which men will live in God as gods, having been raised from the dead. This is a God and His promise so incredible to the ordinary human understanding that, once having believed it, men who reject it can never believe anything else to be of any great value. A world from which such a God has been removed, a man in whom such a hope has been extinguished—are, indeed, in the eyes of those who have undergone such disillusionment, "absurd."

"God is dead," "there is no truth": the two phrases have precisely the same meaning; they are alike a revelation of the absolute absurdity of a world whose center is no longer God, but—nothing. But just here at the very heart of absurdism, its dependence upon the Christianity it rejects is most apparent. One of the most difficult of Christian doctrines for the non-Christian and anti Christian to understand and accept is that of the *creatio ex nihilo:* God's creation of the world not out of Himself, not out of some pre-existent matter, but out of *nothing.* Yet, without understanding it, the absurdist testifies to its reality by inverting and parodying it, by attempting in effect, a nihilization of creation, a return of the world to that very nothingness out of which God first called it. This may be seen in the absurdist affirmation of a void at the center of things, and in the implication present in all absurdists to a greater or lesser degree, that it would be better if man and his world did not exist at all. But this attempt at nihilization, this affirmation of the Abyss, that lies at the very heart of absurdism, takes its most concrete form in the atmosphere that pervades absurdist works of art. In the art of those whom one might call commonplace atheists—men like Hemmingway, Camus, and the vast numbers of artists whose insight does not go beyond the futility of the human situation as men imagine it today, and whose aspiration does not look beyond a kind of stoicism, a facing of the inevitable—in the art of such men the atmosphere of the void is communicated by boredom, by a despair that is yet tolerable, and in general by the feeling that "nothing ever happens." But there is a second, and more revealing, kind of absurdist art, which unites to the mood of futility an element of the unknown, a kind of eerie expectancy, the feeling that in an absurd world, where, generally, "nothing ever happens," it is also true that "anything is possible." In this art, reality becomes a nightmare and the world becomes an alien planet wherein men wander not so much in hopelessness as in perplexity, uncertain of where they are, of what they may find, of their own identity—of everything except the absence of God. This is the strange world of Kafka, of the plays of Ionesco and—less strikingly—of Beckett, of a few avant-garde films like "Last Year at Marienbad," of electronic and other "experimental" music, of surrealism in all the arts, and of the most recent painting and sculpture—and particularly that with a supposedly "religious" content—in which man is depicted as a subhuman or demonic creature emerging from some unknown depths. It was the world, too, of Hitler, whose reign was the most perfect political incarnation we have yet seen of the philosophy of the absurd.

This strange atmosphere is the "death of God" made tangible. It is significant that Nietzsche, in the very passage (in the *Joyful Wisdom*) where he first proclaims the "death of God"—a message he puts in the mouth of a madman—describes the very atmosphere of this absurdist art.

> We have killed him (God), you and I! We are all his murderers! But how have we done it? How were we able to drink up the sea? Who gave us the sponge to wipe away the whole horizon? What did we do when we loosened this earth from its sun? Whither does it now move? Whither do we move? Away from all suns? Do we not dash on unceasingly? Backwards, sideways, forwards, in all directions? Is there still an above and below? Do we not stray, as through infi-

nite nothingness? Does not empty space breathe upon us? Has it
not become colder? Does not night come on continually, darker
and darker?

Such, in fact, is the landscape of the absurd, a landscape in which there
is neither up nor down, right nor wrong, true nor false, because there is
no longer any commonly accepted point of orientation.

Another, more immediately personal, expression of the absurdist
revelation is contained in the despairing cry of Ivan Karamazov: "If
there is no immortality, everything is permitted." This, to some, may
sound like a cry of liberation; but anyone who has thought deeply
about death, or who has encountered, in his own experience, a concrete awareness of his own impending death, knows better that that.
The absurdist, though he denies human immortality, at least recognizes that the question is a central one—something most humanists,
with their endless evasions and rationalizations, fail to do. It is possible
to be indifferent to this question only if one has no love for truth, or if
one's love for truth has been obscured by more deceptive and immediate things, whether pleasure, business, culture, worldly knowledge, or
any of the other things the world is content to accept in place of truth.
The whole meaning of human life depends on the truth—or fal-
sity—of the doctrine of human immortality.

To the absurdist, the doctrine is false. And that is one the reasons
why his universe is so strange: there is no hope in it, death is its highest
god. Apologists for the absurd, like apologists for humanist stoicism,
see nothing but "courage" in this view, the "courage" of men willing to
live without the ultimate "consolation" of eternal life; and they look
down on those who require the "reward" of Heaven to justify their
conduct on earth. It is not necessary, so they think, to believe in
Heaven and Hell in order to lead a "good life" in this world. And their
argument is a persuasive one even to many who call themselves Christians and are yet quite ready to renounce eternal life for an "existential"
view that believes only in the present moment.

Such an argument is the worst of self-deceptions, it is but another of the myriad masks behind which men hide the face of death; for if death were truly the end of men, no man could face the full terror of it. Dostoevsky was quite right in giving to human immortality such central importance in his own Christian world-view. If man is after all to end in nothingness, then in the deepest sense it does not matter what he does in this life, for then nothing he may do is of any ultimate consequence, and all talk of "living this life to the full" is empty and vain. It is absolutely true that if "there is no immortality", the world is absurd and "everything is permitted"—which is to say, nothing is worth doing, the dust of death smothers every joy and prevents even tears, which would be futile; it would indeed be better if such a world did not exist. Nothing in the world—not love, not goodness, not sanctity—is of any value, or indeed even has any meaning, if man does not survive death. He who thinks to lead a "good life" that ends in death does not know the meaning of his words, they but caricature Christian goodness, which finds its fulfillment in eternity. Only if man is immortal, and only if the next world is as God has revealed it to His chosen people, Christians, is there any value or meaning to what man does in this life; for then every act of man is a seed of good or evil that sprouts, to be sure, in this life, but which is not reaped until the future life. Men who, on the other hand, believe that virtue begins and ends in this life are but one step from those who believe that there is no virtue at all; and this step—a fact of which our century bears eloquent witness—is all too easily taken, for it is, after all, a logical step.

Disillusionment, in a sense, is preferable to self-deception. It may, if taken as an end in itself, lead to suicide or madness; but it may also lead to an awakening. Europe for five centuries and more has been deceiving itself, trying to establish a reign of humanism, liberalism, and supposedly Christian values on the basis of an increasingly sceptical attitude toward Christian truth. Absurdism is the end of that road; it is the logical conclusion of the humanist attempt to soften and compromise Christian truth so as to accommodate new, modern, that is to say, worldly, values. Absurdism is the last proof that Christian truth is absolute and uncompromising, or else it is the same as no truth at all; and if there is no truth, if Christian truth is not to be understood literally and absolutely, if God is dead, if there is no immortality—then this world is all there is, and this world is absurd, this world is Hell.

The absurd view of life, then, does express a partial insight: it draws the conclusions of humanist and liberal thought to which well-meaning humanists themselves have been blind. Absurdism is no merely arbitrary irrationalism, but a part of the harvest European man has been sowing for centuries, by his compromise and betrayal of Christian truth.

It would be unwise, however, to exaggerate in this direction, as apologists for the absurd, and to see in absurdism and its parent nihilism signs of a turn or a return to hitherto neglected truths or to a more profound world-view. The absurdist, to be sure, is more realistic about the negative and evil side of life, as manifest both in the world and in man's nature; but this is after all very little truth in comparison with the great errors absurdism shares with humanism. Both are equally far from the God in Whom alone the world makes sense; neither consequently has any notion of spiritual life or experience, which are nourished by God alone; both therefore are totally ignorant of the full dimensions of reality and of human experience; and both have thus a radically oversimplified view of the world and especially of human nature. Humanism and absurdism, in fact, are not as far apart as one might have supposed; absurdism, in the end, is simply disillusioned but unrepentant humanism. It is, one might say, the last stage in the dialectical procession of humanism away from Christian truth, the stage in which humanism, merely by following its internal logic and drawing out the full implications of its original betrayal of Christian truth, arrives at its own negation and ends in a kind of humanist nightmare, a sub-humanism. The subhuman world of the absurdist, though it may at times seem eerie and bewildering, is after all the same one-dimensional world the humanist knows, only rendered "mysterious" by various tricks and self-deceptions; it is a parody of the true world, the world the Christian knows, the world that is truly mysterious because it contains heights and depths of which no absurdist, and surely no humanist, even dreams.

If, intellectually, humanism and absurdism are distinguished as principle and consequence, they are united in a deeper sense, for they share a single will, and that will is the annihilation of the Christian God and the order He has established in the world. These words will seem strange to anyone disposed to take a sympathetic view of the "plight" of contemporary man, and especially to those who listen to the arguments of absurdist apologetics which cite supposed scientific "discoveries" and the all-too-natural disillusionment that has come out of our century of war and revolution: arguments, in short, that rely on the "spirit of the age," which seem to make any but a philosophy of absurdity next to impossible. The universe, so this apology runs, has become meaningless, God has died, one knows not quite how or why, and all we can do now is to accept the fact and resign ourselves to it. But the more perceptive absurdists themselves know better. God has not merely died, said Nietzsche, rather men have murdered Him; and Ionesco, in an essay on Kafka, recognizes that "if man no longer has a guiding thread (i.e., in the labyrinth of life), it is because he no longer wanted to have one. Hence his feeling of guilt, of anxiety, of the absurdity of history." A vague feeling of guilt is indeed, in many cases, the only remaining sign of man's involvement in bringing about the condition in which he now finds himself. But man *is* involved, and all fatalism is only rationalization. Modern science is quite innocent in this respect, for in itself it must be, not merely neutral, but actively hostile to any idea of ultimate absurdity, and those who exploit it for irrationalist ends are not thinking clearly. And as to the fatalism of those who believe that man must be a slave to the "spirit of the age," it is disproved by the experience of every Christian worthy of the name—for the Christian life is nothing if it is not a struggle against the spirit of *every* age for the sake of eternity. Absurdist fatalism is in the end the product, not of knowledge nor of any necessity, but of blind faith. The absurdist, of course, would rather not face too squarely the fact that his disillusionment is an act of faith, for faith is a factor that testifies against determinism. But there is something even deeper than faith which the absurdist has even more reason to avoid, and that is the will; for the direction of a man's will is what chiefly determines his faith and the whole personal world-view built upon that faith. The Christian, who possesses a coherent doctrine of the nature of man and should have thereby a deep insight into human motives, can see the ultimate responsibility the absurdist prefers to deny in his disillusioned view of the world. The absurdist is not the passive "victim" of his age or its thought, but rather an active—though often confused—collaborator in the great undertaking of the enemies of God. Absurdism is not primarily a phenomenon of the intellect, not simple atheism nor mere recognition of the fact of an absent God—these are its disguises and rationalizations; it is rather something of the will, an anti-theism (a term applied by Proudhon to his own program, and seen by de Lubac, in *The Drama of Atheist Humanism,* as a key to understanding other revolutionaries), a fight against God and the Divine order of things. No absurdist, to be sure, can be fully aware of this; he cannot and will not think clearly, he lives on self-delusion. No one (unless it be Satan himself, the first absurdist) can deny God and refuse his own truest happiness in full consciousness of the fact; but somewhere deep within every absurdist, far deeper than he himself usually wishes to look, lies the primordial refusal of God which has been responsible for all the phenomena of absurdism as well as for the incoherence that indeed lies at the very heart of this age.

If it is impossible not to sympathize with some at least of the artists of the absurd, seeing in them an agonized awareness and sincere depiction of a world that is trying to live without God, let us not for all that forget how thoroughly at one these artists are with the world they depict; let us not lose sight of the fact that their art is so successful in striking a responsive chord in many precisely because they share the errors, the blindness and ignorance, and the perverted will of the age whose emptiness they depict. To transcend the absurdity of the contemporary world requires, unfortunately, a great deal more than even the best intentions, the most agonized suffering, and the greatest artistic "genius". The way beyond the absurd lies in truth alone; and this is precisely what is lacking as much in the contemporary artist as in his world, it is what is actively rejected as definitely by the self-conscious absurdist as it is by those who live the absurd life without being aware of it. To sum up, then, our diagnosis of absurdism: it is the life lived, and the view of live expressed, by those who can or will no longer see God as the beginning and end, and the ultimate meaning, of life; those who therefore do not believe His Revelation of Himself in Jesus Christ and do not accept the eternal Kingdom He has prepared for those who do believe and who live this faith; those who, ultimately, can hold no one responsible for their unbelief but themselves. But what is the *cause* of this disease? What, beyond all historical and psychological causes—which can never be more than relative and contributory—what is its real motivation, its spiritual cause? If absurdism is indeed a great evil, as we believe it to be, it cannot be chosen for its own sake; for evil has no positive existence, and it can only be chosen in the guise of a seeming good. If up to this point we have described the negative side of the philosophy of the absurd, its description of the disordered, disoriented world in which men find themselves today, it is time to turn to its positive side and discover in what it is that absurdists place their faith and hope.

For it is quite clear that absurdists are not happy about the absurdity of the universe; they believe in it, but they cannot reconcile themselves to it, and their art and thought are attempts, after all, to transcend it. As Ionesco has said (and here he speaks, probably, for all absurdists): "To attack absurdity is a way of stating the possibility of non-absurdity," and he sees himself as engaged in "the constant search for an opening, a revelation." Thus we return to the sense of expectancy we have already noted in certain absurdist works of art; it is but a reflection of the situation of our times, wherein men, disillusioned and desolate, yet hope in something unknown, uncertain, yet to be revealed, which will somehow restore meaning and pupose to life. Men cannot live without hope, even in the midst of despair, even when all cause for hope has been, supposedly, "disproved."

But this is only to say that nothingness, the apparent center of the absurdist universe, is not the real heart of the disease, but only its most striking symptom. The real faith of absurdism is in something hoped for but not yet fully manifest, a "Godot" that is the always implicit but not yet defined subject of absurdist art, a mysterious something that, if understood, would give life some kind of meaning once more.

All this, if it seems vague in contemporary absurdist art, is quite clear in the works of the original "prophets" of the age of absurdity, Nietzsche and Dostoevsky. In them the revelation of absurdity has a corollary. "Dead are all the gods," says Nietzsche's Zarathustra: "Now do we desire the Superman to live." And Nietzsche's madman says, of the murder of God: "Is not the magnitude of this deed too great for us? Shall we not ourselves have to become gods, merely to seem worthy of it?" Kirillov, in Dostoevsky's *Possessed,* knows that, "If there is no God, then I am God."

Man's first sin, and the ultimate cause of the miserable condition of man in all ages, was in following the temptation of the serpent in Paradise: "Ye shall be as gods." What Nietzsche calls the Superman, and Dostoevsky the man-god, is in fact the same god of *self* with which the Devil then, and always, has tempted man; it is the only god, once the true God has been rejected, whom men can worship. Man's freedom has been given him to choose between the true God and himself, between the true path to deification whereon the self is humbled and crucified in this life to be resurrected and exalted in God in eternity, and the false path of self-deification which promises exaltation in this life but ends in the Abyss. These are the only two choices, ultimately, open to the freedom of man; and upon them have been founded the two Kingdoms, the Kingdom of God and the Kingdom of Man, which may be discriminated only by the eye of faith in this life, but which shall be separated in the future life as Heaven and Hell. It is clear to which of them modern civilization belongs, with its Promethean effort to build a Kingdom of earth in defiance of God; but what should be clear enough in earlier modern thinkers becomes absolutely explicit in Nietzsche. The old commandment of "Thou shalt," says Zarathustra, has become outmoded; the new commandment is "I will". And in Kirillov's satanic logic, "The attribute of my godhead is self-will." The new religion, the religion not yet fully revealed that will succeed the old religion of Christianity to which modern man thinks by now to have delivered the final blow—is supremely the religion of self-worship.

This is what absurdism—and all the vain experimentation of our day—is seeking. Absurdism is the stage at which the modern Promethean effort hesitates, entertains doubts, and has a faint foretaste of the satanic incoherence in which it cannot but end. But if the absurdist is less confident and more fearful than the humanist, he nonetheless shares the humanist faith that the modern path is the right path, and in spite of his doubt be retains the humanist hope—hope not in God and His Kingdom, but in man's own Tower of Babel.

The modern attempt to establish a kingdom of self-worship reached one extreme in Hitler, who believed in a racial Superman; it reaches another extreme in Communism, whose Superman is the collectivity and whose self-love is disguised as altruism. But both Naziism and Communism are extreme forms—their phenomenal success proves it—of what everyone else today actually believes: everyone, that is, who does not stand explicitly and absolutely with Christ and His Truth. For what is the meaning of the gigantic effort in which all nations have today joined to transform the face of the earth and conquer the universe, to bring about an entirely new order of things wherein man's condition since his creation will be radically transformed and this earth, which since man's fall has been and can be nothing but a place of sorrow and tears, is to become, supposedly, a place of happiness and joy, a veritable heaven on earth with the advent of a "new age"? What does this mean but that man, freed of the burden of a God in Whom he does not believe even when he professes Him with his lips, imagines himself to be God, master of his own destiny and creator of a "new earth," expressing his faith in a "new religion" of his own devising wherein humility gives way to pride, prayer to worldly knowledge, mastery of the passions to mastery of the world, fasting to abundance and satiety, tears of repentance to worldly joy.

To this religion of the self absurdism points the way. This is not, to be sure, always its explicit intention, but it is its distinct implication. Absurdist art depicts a man imprisoned in his own self, unable to communicate with his fellow man or enter into any relationship with him that is not inhuman; there is no love in absurdist art, there is only hatred, violence, terror, and boredom—because in cutting himself off from God, absurdist man has cut himself off from his own humanity, the image of God. If such a man is awaiting a revelation that will put an end to absurdity, it is surely not the revelation that the Christians know; if there is one point on which all absurdists would agree, it is the absolute rejection of the Christian answer. Any revelation the absurdist, as absurdist, can accept must be "new." About Godot, in Beckett's play, one character says, "I'm anxious to hear what he has to offer. Then we'll take it or leave it." In the Christian life everything is referred to Christ, the old self with its constant "I will" must be done away with and a new self, centered in Christ and His will, be born; but in the spiritual universe of "Godot," everything revolves precisely about the old self, and even a new god must present himself as a kind of spiritual merchandise to be accepted or rejected by a self that will tolerate nothing that is not oriented to itself. Men today "wait for Godot"—who is, perhaps on one level, Antichrist—in the hope that he will bring appeasement of conscience and restore meaning and joy to self-worship, in the hope that is, that he will permit what God has forbidden and provide the ultimate apology for it. Nietzsche's Superman is absurdist, modern man with his sense of guilt obliterated in a frenzy of enthusiasm generated by a false mysticism of the earth, a worship of this world.

Where will it all end? Nietzsche and the optimists of our day see the dawn of a new age, the beginning of "a higher history than any history hitherto." Communist doctrine affirms this; but the Communist reorganization of the world will, in the end, prove to be no more than the systematized absurdity of a perfectly efficient machine that has no ultimate purpose. Dostoevsky, who knew the true God, was more realistic. Kirillov, the maniacal counterpart of Zarathustra, had to kill himself to prove that he was God; Ivan Karamazov, who was tormented by the same ideas, ended in madness, as did Nietzsche himself; Shigalev (in *The Possessed*), who devised the first perfect social organization of mankind, found it necessary to deliver nine-tenths of mankind to absolute slavery so that one-tenth might enjoy absolute liberty—a plan that Nazi and Communist Supermen have put into practice. Madness, suicide, slavery, murder, and destruction are the ends of the presumptuous philosophy of the death of God and the advent of the Superman; and these are, indeed, prominent themes of absurdist art.

Many feel—with Ionesco—that only out of thorough exploration of the absurd condition in which man now finds himself, and of the new possibilities this has opened up for him, may a way be found beyond absurdity and nihilism into some new realm of coherence: this is the hope of absurdism and humanism, and it will become the hope of Communism when (and if) it enters its period of disillusionment. It is a false hope, but it is a hope that may, for all that, be fulfilled. For Satan is the ape of God, and once divine coherence has been shattered and men no longer hope for the absolute coherence God alone can give to human life, the counterfeit coherence that Satan is able to fabricate may come to seem quite attractive. It is no accident that in our own day serious attention is being given once more by responsible and sober Christians dissatisfied alike with facile optimism and facile pessimism, to a doctrine that, in Western Europe at least, was almost forgotten for centuries under the influence of the philosophy of enlightenment and progress. (Cf. Josef Pieper, *The End of Time*; Heinrich Schlier, *Principalities and Powers in the New Testament*; and before them, Cardinal Newman.) This is the doctrine, universally held by the Churches of the East and West, of Antichrist, that strange figure who appears at the end of time as a humanitarian world-ruler and seems to turn creation upside-down by making darkness seem light, evil good, slavery freedom, chaos order; he is the ultimate protagonist of the philosophy of the absurd, and the perfect embodiment of the man-god: for he will worship only himself, and will call himself God. This is no place, however, to do more than point out the existence of that doctrine, and to note its intimate connection with the Satanic incoherence of the philosophy of the absurd.

But more important even than the historical culmination of absurdism, whether it be the actual reign of Antichrist or merely another of his predecessors, is its supra-historical end: and that is Hell. For absurdism is, most profoundly, an irruption of Hell into our world; it is thus a warning of a reality men are all too anxious to avoid. But those who avoid it only find themselves the closer to it; our age, the first in Christian times to disbelieve entirely in Hell, itself more thoroughly than any other embodies the spirit of Hell.

Why do men disbelieve in Hell? It is because they do not believe in Heaven, i.e., because they do not believe in life, and in the God of life, because they find God's creation absurd and wish that it did not exist. The Starets Zossima, in *The Brothers Karamazov,* speaks of one kind of such men.

> There are some who remain proud and fierce even in hell.... They have cursed themselves, cursing God and life.... They cannot behold the living God without hatred, and they cry out that the God of life should be annihilated, that God should destroy Himself and His own creation. And they will burn in the fire of their own wrath for ever and yearn for death and annihilation. But they will not attain to death....

Such men, of course, are extreme nihilists, but they differ in degree only, and not in kind, from those less violent souls who faintly curse this life and find it to be absurd, and even from those who call themselves Christians and do not desire the Kingdom of Heaven with all their hearts, but picture Heaven, if at all, as a shadowy realm of repose or sleep. Hell is the answer and the end of all who believe in death rather than life, in this world rather than in the next world, in themselves rather than in God: all those, in short, who in their deepest heart accept the philosophy of the absurd. For it is the great truth of Christianity—which Dostoevsky saw and Nietzsche did not see—that *there is no annihilation,* and *there is no incoherence,* all nihilism and absurdism are in vain. The flames of Hell are the last and awful proof of this: every creature testifies, with or against his will, to the ultimate coherence of things. For this coherence is the love of God, and this love is found even in the flames of Hell; it is in fact the love of God itself which torments those who refuse it.

So it is too with absurdism; it is the negative side of a positive reality. There is, of course, an element of incoherence in our world, for in his fall from Paradise man brought the world with him; the philosophy of the absurd is not, therefore, founded upon a total lie, but upon a deceptive half-truth. But when Camus defines absurdity as the confrontation of man's need for reason with the irrationality of the world, when he believes that man is an innocent victim and the world the guilty party, he, like all absurdists, has magnified a very partial insight into a totally distorted view of things, and in his blindness has arrived at the exact inversion of the truth. Absurdism, in the end, is an *internal* and not an external question; it is not the world that is irrational and incoherent, but man.

If, however, the absurdist is responsible for not seeing things as they are, and not even wishing to see things as they are, the Christian is yet more responsible for failing to give the example of a fully coherent life, a life in Christ. Christian compromise in thought and word and negligence in deed have opened the way to the triumph of the forces of the absurd, of Satan, of Antichrist. The present age of absurdity is the just reward of Christians who have failed to be Christians.

And the only remedy for absurdism lies at this, its source: we must again be Christians. Camus was quite right when he said, "We must choose between miracles and the absurd." For in this respect Christianity and absurdism are equally opposed to Enlightenment rationalism and humanism, to the view that reality can be reduced to purely rational and human terms. We must indeed choose between the miraculous, the Christian view of things, whose center is God and whose end is the eternal Kingdom of Heaven, and the absurd, the Satanic view of things, whose center is the fallen self and whose end is Hell, in this life and in the life to come.

We must again be Christians. It is futile, in fact it is precisely absurd, to speak of reforming society, of changing the path of history, of emerging into an age beyond absurdity, if we have not Christ in our hearts; and if we do have Christ in our hearts, nothing else matters.

It is of course possible that there may be an age beyond absurdity; it is more likely, perhaps—and Christians must always be prepared for this eventuality—that there will not be, and that the age of absurdity is indeed the last age. It may be that the final testimony Christians may be able to give in this age will be the ultimate testimony, the blood of their martyrdom.

But this is cause for rejoicing and not for despair. For the hope of Christians is not in this world or in any of its kingdoms—that hope, indeed, is the ultimate absurdity; the hope of Christians is in the Kingdom of God which is not of this world.

Since 1965, the St. Herman of Alaska Brotherhood has been publishing Orthodox Christian books and magazines.

View our catalog, featuring over sixty titles, and order online, at
www.sainthermanmonastery.com

You can also write us for a free printout of our catalog:

St. Herman of Alaska Brotherhood
P. O. Box 70
Platina, CA 96076
USA